One Soft Whisper

"I will put my spirit in you that you may live, and I will settle you upon your land; thus, you shall know that I am the Lord. I have promised and I will do it, says the Lord." (Ezekiel 37: 12b-14).

Dedication

My dedication of these writings must be and is with the deepest devotion.

I first and foremost dedicate these writings and giggles to my dear sister Barbara. Her life was not easy, but she endured and never lost the love and deep concerns for the well-being of others. She was the epitome of what love is all about.

I also dedicate these words and the effort to Rev. A.G. Wagner, Sister Angela, George and Margaret Mayerchak, Robert Sweitzer, John and Amelia Comrie, Fred McNeary, Dr. Mastrioni, Bill and Gerry Dorey, Bill and Lena McPhearson, Bill and Loretta Collins, Fred and Edna Buckreis, Wanda Hodge, Carl Hendren, Mnsgr. Theo Sherotti, Dr Satchetelli, Dr. Jeremy Tarter, Dr, Robert Hendrickson, Ann Greenwell, Emma Shannon, Sid and Helen Hill, Jerry and Carol Lunney, Kevin Kreuger, Rev. Walter Bado SJ, Dc Dennis Chatham, Randy and Lisa Schneider, Rev. Alan Carter, Charlotte Henson, Tom and Holly Hanson, Rebecca Rowe, Judy Vick, Ralph Clark, Paul Stansbury.

These angels sent to me from God held onto my bib straps and did not let me slip away. They included me and taught me what loving self, and another is all about.

Cover design by Twanda Smith.

All Bible references taken from: The Holy Bible King James Version 1982; The Holy Bible New Catholic Edition 1962; New American Bible 1970

Table of Contents

Foreword

When Twanda asked me to write this intro to her book, I thought where to start? How do you find over ten years of friendship into a few pages? So, I thought why not start at the beginning?

I had seen Twanda frequently around church, even said hello, but it was about a year before I sat down and had a conversation with her as she watched the children play in the Methodist Church nursery. I can't say what it was that let me know I could trust her or even what prompted me to talk to her. Perhaps, at some point in the past year of passing her in the halls, I noticed a kindred spirit. Perhaps it was how she interacted and laughed with the kids. When I saw her dressed up like a clown painting faces at the Fall Festival I, at least, knew she had a sense of humor and adventure. I don't remember how long we talked or even what we talked about that Sunday morning. What I do remember is how she made me feel. I felt accepted for who I was, no matter what, and that she actually cared to listen. Two things which are very important for a teenager. The friendship that blossomed from that conversation has been one that has helped me through many dark and difficult places as well as walked with me through many joyful experiences.

There were many Sunday mornings that we would spend the time between Sunday school and Sunday Service, chatting and laughing in the nursery. It was always the highlight of my Sunday morning. After Twanda returned to the Catholic Church we lost contact for a couple of years until I showed up on her doorstep one afternoon. I had just had my whole world flipped upside down and shattered by some of the very same people who had caused her to leave the Methodist Church. I don't know how I even knew where she lived or what made me think of her when the rest of the world seemed to have abandoned me. But I remembered those Sunday mornings.

"I need to talk." I said. She didn't ask questions, all she said was "Okay, come in." as she ushered me into her kitchen. For the next two hours she listened, patiently, as I poured out everything I had been going through: the betrayal I felt, the anger, the sadness. All she did was listen, but listen was all I needed.

After that I was a regular at Twanda's house, every Sunday evening for two years we had supper, sitting in the backyard or watching old movies. Afterwards we would stay up until midnight, one o'clock just talking. During the summer of 2009 we built and wired a wall for her carport. A favorite memory is sitting under that carport during a thunderstorm. The rain was coming down but did nothing to dampen our spirits. During one lull in the conversation we sat quietly listening to the rain and watching it hit the driveway. When all of a sudden a bolt of lightning came out of the sky and hit the manhole cover in the road, not fifteen feet from where we were sitting. Blue sparks danced across the pavement and sound like a cannon echoed through the air. Twanda looked at me and I looked at her, both of us with equal surprise. "I think we'd better go in." She said. "Yup." Was all I said as I stood up and we headed into the house.

Twanda grew in me an appreciation for many kinds of music, from classical to the '50's and '60's. Sometimes she would call me about a Southern Gospel Concert she had heard about and together we would go and listen to the performance.

Twanda taught me to take care of plants and love nature, teaching me to garden in her backyard, which she had turned into the American equivalent of an English Victorian paradise. It was a place of magic for me, an escape from the outside world. Whether we were planting or weeding or going out into the country to collect geodes to decorate, I loved that garden. One summer she asked me to help prune the pear tree because it was so heavy with fruit the branches were ready to break. I was up on the ladder cutting through a limb while she held another offshoot out of the way. Over the sound of the chainsaw, we heard a loud crack and the branch gave way, pulling the ladder out from underneath me. The chainsaw landed a fair distance away and I managed to grab a nearby branch so that as I fell, I swung so as to avoid being impaled by the brush below me. When I came up from amongst the branches I began to laugh at how ridiculous the whole situation was. Once she realized I was alright, she began to laugh too. I had leaves sticking out of my hair, my clothes were rumpled and dirty; I looked like a young Rip Van Winkle coming up out of the brush.

When I went off to college, I would always visit when I came home, Sunday nights would find me again at her place, laughing and listening. She had the most amazing stories to tell, about growing up in the mountains, about her travels and the people she met, the research into genealogy she had done, and about raising her family, whom she still loved very much. Sometimes she would repeat stories, but I never minded because they were always the same and always just as good. In many ways she became a grandmother to me, since my own has always lived too far away for a quick visit. Today, every time I go home, Twanda's is still a place I make a point of visiting.

As you read this book, don't just read it like another story; allow its contents to teach you what the author has taught me. She taught me many things about living, laughing and being happy. She taught me how to make the most out of what I am given and to always look for the bright side of a situation. She taught me to never turn away someone at the door, to always listen to others and never say something about someone you wouldn't say to their face, to own up to the consequences of your actions and to *illegitimi non carborundum*. For the rest of my life there will be many things I remember about Twanda, but something I will always remember is how she made that teenage boy feel on a Sunday morning when he was feeling alone, and how she has made him feel ever since.

Seth Slone, Seminarian

A Misty Morning

It was a misty morning with a heavy dew on the grass. She drew her first breath at 5:45am. She came into the world screaming and wailing as loud as a banshee. The first three years of her life was filled with much laughter, many hugs and lots and lots of love. She in fact was a spoiled rotten brat.

The little girl's mother was a believer. The mother was sickly and had been since the age of nine. At that time, she had become ill with strep throat, which was not treated, and her heart became damaged with Rheumatic heart. She was virtually an invalid from that day until the day she died. Her daddy adored her as he did his other two children and doted on them. But, to the middle and sick one, he devoted his life. She had medical specialists in a town two hundred miles away. He worked as a machinist in the local coal mines. He would drive her to the doctor every time she had to go. They were faithful, went to church, prayed and took joy in helping those less fortunate.

The stories carried down through the years were that the mother would get on her knees and pray for long periods of time. They said that she would pray, and weep and the water would run down her cheeks and drip onto the floor. They said that you could see a puddle around her on the floor. Some said that she was filled with such guilt about having brought the two children into the world, was overpowering to her. She knew that she would not live to see them grow up and she turned to God. Her father passed away three months before her. He had a stroke and went blind from it. He walked to and from work for nine days before someone became aware of his loss of vision.

“Fear not for I am with you. I am the Lord your God.” (Isaiah 43)

When She Was Three Years Old

When she was three years old, she went into the living room of her grandmother's house and saw a big box setting in front of the window. She pulled a chair over to the box and peeked in. Her mother was sleeping. She couldn't wake her mother and when she touched her face it was cold and hard. She tried again to wake her but could not. She crawled up the stairs to the bedroom of her grandmother and drug a blanket down the stairs and over to the big box. She climbed upon the chair and pushed and pulled the blanket over onto her mother. She climbed into the box beside her mother thinking that she could warm her up, if she could get her warm, she would hug her close and talk to her, as she always did. She, herself got warm and fell asleep. She awoke to shouting and screaming with the room filled with her family. All the commotion scared her, and she cried. Her Daddy picked her up and held her close to his body, He was so warm and smelled good. She snuggled into him and still being scared of all the shouting, did stop crying. She did not know what she had done wrong. Her daddy kept saying "there there now, it is ok, you did nothing wrong. It is OK". After that day she went into the big box many times, but someone always followed after her. They would not let her get into the box again, her mother never moved or got out of the box. Sometime after that she was standing beside a big hole in the ground and the big box was setting on top of the hole. She could not see what was keeping the box from falling into the hole. Maybe all the crying and talking was keeping it from falling. They took the pretty flowers off the top of the box and then the box was going down into the hole. Did they take out her mother before they did that? Where was she? Where was her mother? Her daddy picked her up and started walking away. She was screaming and crying. Where was her mother? Everyone just sat around and cried or talked. They did not go to work, or church. Things sure were not happy anymore.

Grandma called to her and asked her to show the man upstairs and show him the little stool in her bedroom. She remembered the stairs and how quickly she reached the top of them.

She looked down and the bottom looked a long way off, and they seemed to be longer. She got her hand back from the man and showed him into her grandma's bedroom. When she got to the little stool, she sat on it. The man sat down on his legs in front of her and was talking. His hand went up into her panties. He kept talking and told her that if she said anything about this, he would hurt her grandma and her sister. His hands and fingers were hurting her. She started to cry. Then it happened. It felt like a tickle, but it was not. It hurt, it felt good. She stopped crying and the man picked her up and was holding her close in his arms. He was telling her to be quiet, to not tell anyone what we had done. He said the boogeyman would come get her if she told about it. The man took the stool with him and left. That day she ran to the living room and sat down in the floor in the rays of sun coming through the window. She cried. She did not tell anyone about the man and what he did. When the man came back with the stool, it had a red cover on it. He asked her to take him to her grandma's room so he could put the stool back where it was. She started crying and ran out the door into the yard. The neighbor was out there, and he picked her up and cuddled her in his arms. He said quiet words to her, and she stopped crying.

“From my pursuer save me and rescue me.” (Psalm 7)

The Older Sister

The older sister had an accident when she was two years old. The cousin had sat her on a swing (a rope dangling from a limb of a tree with a board balanced between the two sides of dangling rope). She was told to hang on tight but with the force of being pushed and not being very strong went flying out of the swing. She landed about 50 feet away down the side of the hill, on the roof of the store below them. She had bad damage to her skull. The doctors did not know what to do. They carried her around sitting on their hip for a long time. She healed but her brain was damaged. She could not grasp learning and was slow.

She did not like the long ride in the car. Daddy just kept driving and driving. They drove up a hill and stopped in front of a house. Two people came out and hugged daddy and cried like the other people did, where they came from. They hugged her and her sister and cried and cried. Daddy was there and then he was in the car and driving away and leaving them behind. Where was he going? Why was he not taking them with him?

She was just a wee tike then, about four years of age. She can remember the blue sky without clouds and listening to the birds chirping all around. They seemed to be louder then. But they skittered to and fro looking for food just as today. She can let her thoughts drift now, but for years she looked back and wept.

She stood in that meadow asking God why her Mother had to go live with Him, when she needed her so much. She could not understand why she would want to go live with Jesus when she was just a little girl and needed her loving arms to hold her tight.

She could not understand why she had to come to this place when she was happy with Granny. She had this Grandma, but she was not loving and caring as her Granny was. This Grandma did not put her arms around her and hold her when she fell and scraped her knee or mashed her fingers in the door. Yes, she gave her attention, when she did something that she did not like, she got a switching, but she was so wanting her to put her arms around her and just hold her, to cuddle her as her Granny did.

Living on the farm with Grandma and Grandpa, Daddy's parents was a lot of hard work and she soon learned that if she stuck close to Grandpa, that she could enjoy some giggles and small pleasures each day. Grandpa knew about all the good things in life, and he shared them with her, He knew where the sweetest peaches where, the ripest apricots (in the pig pen) were and he could choose the most, bestest apple on the tree. His biggie in the summer months was to pluck a melon from the patch and lay it in the cool water of the creek and when they were hot and sweaty from working the fields, they would smash that melon and eat the sweet meat. He knew that if you were slow and could keep your mouth shut you could catch a fish, or a frog, or a rabbit. She loved learning from him and learned quickly.

Grandpa was always asking her to do something for him and that made her feel special. He would give her little chores to do to keep her busy. A lot of the things that were given to her to do required common sense to accomplish. These turned out to be most valuable

There were animals just about everywhere. Cows horses, pigs, chickens. Everywhere she went there was an animal to hug and play with. The man gave her the job of feeding the animals. That was fun. She shelled the corn off the cob, and they ate it off her hand. They followed her around everywhere. The man told her that he was her grandpa and that he wanted her to call him grandpa.

She herself followed him every step he took. It was surely much better to follow him around than stay at the house where the woman hollered and made her do things in the house. Why should she have to wipe the dust off the tables when the next day she had to do it all over again. Yes, being with the animals was more fun than chasing all that dust around.

The grandmother had an open seeping wound on the right side of her forehead. She had it from the day she married grandpa. From what was gleaned in later years, that marriage was not sanctioned by the church as it came about due to pregnancy from rape without marriage. The woman was of Native descent and some things were just not looked upon favorably in the village. It is said that the young boy that committed the offense was visited by the village elders and "put" in his place.

“Lord be gracious to us; for You we wait. Be our strength every morning, our salvation in time of trouble.” (Isaiah 33:2)

There Was a Litter of Pigs

There was a litter of pigs born. That was the most exciting thing she had ever seen. They just kept popping out of the big sow. Grandpa picked up one of the little pigs and said, "This one will have to go, it is too little”. She wanted to hold it and he handed it to her. He was so cute, and he squeaked. Grandpa wanted to take it back, he said that he had to kill it. She screamed hollered; she ran. He was not going to kill this little pig. It was just a baby. Grandpa went back to work and soon she had to go help feed. He told her the little pig was too small and he had to kill it because it would never be worth anything. She would not give it up. She begged, cried, and begged some more. She told him that she would feed it, she would take care of it. The next day Grandpa told her that she could keep the pig, but she had to be sure to feed it and take care of it. The first thing she did, was give it a bath. After that she and the little pig. were together constantly. She named him ‘Porky’ She would sneak him into the house and cuddle him ‘under the covers of her pad. She and her sister slept on the floor of the feed room in the house. There was always corn, and feed dropped on the floor. Little mice would come out at night and eat. They would carry food with them, and then come back for more. Porky loved being in the room also, he would eat his fill of the food dropped on the floor. She liked it that way. With them eating, she never had to sweep it up.

On Saturday while getting set to go to town, she was helping grandpa put the milk and stuff onto the truck. She asked if she could take Porky with them to town. Grandpa laughed and said "no, of course not" Then she reminded him that Porky was like a dog and he would behave. He stood on one foot, one on the running board and looked down at Porky. Porky seemed to know what was at hand and he Squealed really loud. Grandpa laughed and said that he could go. Porky sat on the seat between them. He sat there and looked out the windows. every now and then he would squeal and shake his head. When they went into Uncle's store to take their wares, Porky walked right along with them just like he had been doing it all along. He stopped in front of Uncle and nodded his head and squealed. Uncle laughed and said, "Welcome little buddy, welcome". After that Porky went with them everywhere they went. The places they went to, the people would speak to Porky and pat him on the head. He loved all the attention. He was her friend and her pal. After a while Porky got too big to get into the front seat, and he traveled in the bed of the truck. Then he got so big he could not get into the bed of the truck and he had to stay in the lot with the other pigs, while they went to town.

"Like the deer that yearns for running streams, so my soul is yearning for you, my God." (Psalm 42)

Life on the farm was a joy. With all the animals and work to do, she was growing tall and strong. She was happy. That was as long as she did not have to stay at the house. She hoed corn. She fed the animals. She helped cut, rake and haul hay. She was the one that went to the big pole stuck into the ground and tramp down the hay around it while the men pitched the hay around the pole. She cleaned stalls in the barn. She milked the cows. She gathered the eggs. She helped haul rock and build up the road again each time it got washed out by the rain. She helped at the sawmill keeping things tidy. She had to keep away from the blades and belts. They were too dangerous for her to be around. She was, however, still with grandpa.

One day while they were sitting on the porch breaking beans, a car drove into the yard. It was Daddy. She fell down the steps trying to rush to get to him. She jumped into his arms the minute he stepped out of the car. He hugged her and kept saying, " I love you, how are you"? Grandma and Grandpa were really glad to see him also. Sister cried and stayed away. Daddy had to go to her and after a while she hugged him. There was a woman in the car. Holy Moly, she was ugly. She had the longest neck she had ever seen except for a cow or horse. Her hair was bright red and stringy, and oily. Her legs were about four feet long. She had no teeth. Her head was too little for her body. Who was she? What was she doing with Daddy? Didn't take long to find out. She was going to be our new mother.

The girl ran and ran in the other direction. Old Betsy, the cow was laying in the grass in the pasture, chewing her cud. She ran to her and fell down beside her. She crawled up as close as she could and cried and cried. The cow seemed to know that she was sad, as she reached around and licked her on the head, and mooed real low. It sounded like it was coming from inside her. She fell asleep and a time later, grandpa was sitting beside her on the grass. He was telling her that she had to be a big girl and listen to her daddy. She was told that she and her sister were going to live with daddy and his new wife. She did not want to do that. She was really happy living with grandpa and grandma. All the tears could not keep her with them, they were in the car and going to live with someone else.

"God is the shield that protects me." (Psalm 7)

When the Girls Got to Daddy's House

When the girls got to Daddy's house things were really strange. Daddy would leave the house and go to work. He would be gone for very long times. While he was gone, things were different. They had to scrub the floors, wash the dishes, scrub the clothes in a wash tub on the back porch with our hands. They could never please her (daddy's wife) because they had to do everything over and over and over. She told them the rules. If daddy was in the room, they could not go into the room. If daddy came into the room where they were, they were to leave the room immediately. They could not hug daddy anymore. He could not hug them. They could only eat what she gave them to eat. They could only sit at the kitchen table and eat when daddy was there, but no other time. They could not drink the milk; it was for daddy. When daddy was around she could hear what they were saying sometimes. His wife was so sweet when he was around. She laughed and loved on him.

If they did something that she did not like, she would hit them with a stick of wood, cut for the wood stove, a broom handle, a yard stick, anything she could get her hands on She would pull them out of bed and beat them with whatever she could get a hold of. They loved it when daddy was around, they were left alone.

The older girl did as she was a told but not much more than that. She spent a lot of time just being and hugging her doll that Granny had given her. Daddy’s wife did not bother with her very much. She just laughed at her and made fun of her. A lot of people made fun of her. She could not learn. The woman would whip her, daddy would whip her. She just could not get it. About that time the girls began to make believe and spent time playing in a make believe world. Little was it known at the time, but the older child began to weave a cocoon about herself. A cocoon that would last for another 69 years of her life

----

“When he was insulted, he returned no insult.” (1 Peter 2:21)

When she was 8 years old, she was sitting on the grass

stringing up clover blooms again and a car drove up and three men got out. They went to our front door and knocked. Daddy came to the door, and they pulled him out of the house and put metal bracelets on him. They put daddy into the car they came in and took off down the street.

Daddy did not come back that night and no one would tell her anything about who the men were and why they took daddy away. That night the woman started screaming and yelling like an idiot. She was running back and forth between the back door, and the front door. There was a bright light coming through the front window. When she went to the window to look out, there was a big cross burning on the front yard. Where did the cross come from? Why were they doing that. There were men there and they had sheets over their heads. They were just standing there watching the cross burn. Then all together they got into cars and trucks and went down the street. The neighbors took down the cross and calmed the woman down. One man kept saying, "you ole witch, they should have taken you". He yelled really loud for her to "shut up and stop squalling". When the girl walked to school the next day, no one even looked at her. Of course, no one spoke to her, because they knew if they spoke to her, that the woman would beat the crap out of her. She never knew why they came and got daddy. She did not know how long he was away. She just knows that the woman did not beat her one time for a long time. Then daddy came home, and she beat her really bad. She could not open her eye for a week, and her nose is crooked to this day.

Her family would come around all the time when daddy was at work. They would laugh, smoke, drink but before daddy got home from work, they would leave. Sometimes they would stay overnight. They slept on the other bed in the same room as her sister and her. She could hear all kinds of things, moaning, rustling about, talking. Just crazy stuff. Sometimes she would awake with someone touching her between her legs. That was when she started dreaming of a big black bear putting his paw up inside her. She would wake so scared and crying. They would stick things up inside her and It would always hurt, and she would cry, but they would not stop. There was no one to talk to. No one to tell. At school one day, she told her teacher that she was hurting between her legs. The teacher said, "Stop peeing your pants".

Daddy went to work, and her people came. They smoked a lot and drank a lot. Daddy kept a glass jar in the refrigerator filled with water. They drank a lot of it that night. They woke her sometime in the night touching her. They had put something in her butt hole, and it was hurting. They put their hand over her mouth to shut her up, she was on her stomach and they kept pushing something into her. She did not remember anything after a while, and it was daylight when she woke up. She had to go to school, or she would get another beating. When she got to school, she had to wash off the blood rolling down her legs.

Sometime later she was walking down the hallway at school and fell asleep. When she woke up she was in the restroom with a teacher. The teacher was washing her legs and her bottom. The teacher asked her how she had hurt herself. She does not know what she said, but when she got home, she was so weak, she fell onto the floor. She woke up being beaten with a stick of wood. The witch was yelling that she would kill her for making her look bad and telling lies at school. The next time that she woke daddy was there, but she could not hear what he was saying.

“Guard me as the apple of your eye, Hide me in the shadow of your wings from the violent attack of the wicked.” (Psalm 17)

Daddy Called Them

Daddy called them into the kitchen, and when they got there, they were told that they were going to another place to live They had been so bad that his wife could not handle them anymore. They went to a house on a mountain outside Bryson City, North Carolina.

* * *

We all wear masks, and the time comes when we cannot remove them without removing our skin. - Twanda

* * *

When they arrived at the house on the side of the mountain, there were four children, pretty children, a woman and a man. They all were beautiful. Their hair was raven black, their skin was olive color, and the eyes, the eyes were almond shaped. They hugged her and laughed. They were so happy to see them.

They were told that they were kin and that the woman and man were Aunt and Uncle; the children were cousins. The house was made of logs. The floors were dirt. The floors were very hard and shiny. There were no beds. There was a table and chairs but little else. At night pads were placed on the floor and bear skin rugs to sleep on. She was told that because she was a bed wetter, a pad was to be placed upon the bear skin to protect it. They were told that they were loved and that they were welcome to be there.

Uncle spent much of his time outdoors. He would bring in some type of meat every day. Aunt stayed at the cabin with the children singing just about constantly. The children played but when it came time to help out, they happily went to work with their mother. There was a very large cleared out area in the midst of the trees, where a large vegetable garden had been planted. The children were helping to keep the garden healthy and growing. Uncle spent a lot of time in the garden working. He too, would sing. Sometimes he would be working in the garden or cutting wood or something else away from the house, Aunt would start a song and the children would join in, then from out there somewhere Uncle would begin to sing with them. It was so beautiful to hear with the sound of them flowing through the trees. It was not long before the girls began to join in and sing right along with them.

Uncle would sit around the outdoor cooking area whittling, working leather or something to keep him busy and he would begin to tell stories to the children. These stories had been handed down through the lines of the elders for centuries. He told them about the Great Spirit coming down from the heavens and teaching the people how to live, how to love, and how to find the way back to the heavens when they died. He told them about the young girl that the Great Spirit had chosen to be the mother of His son on earth. He told them of the rules that the Great Spirit had given to his helpers on earth, in order that they could live by the rules and live good lives. These stories were told every day around the fire. Uncle told other stories also. They heard about their kin that had lived before and the good they did while they lived on the earth.

One very sun filled morning while the dew was still burning off the trees and grass, three young men walked out of the trees into the clearing of the cabin. They were hiking and asked if they could cross the land. Uncle greeted them and asked them to sit for a while and eat some food. They all sat around the outdoor fire pit and Aunt made them breakfast. They sat with Uncle a long time. The children were permitted to come sit for a while.

When Uncle and Aunt came to the mountain to live a young bear cub was orphaned by hunters killing the mother. Uncle raised the cub and they became lasting friends. The cub grew and became an adult bear. She was big. She would come back to visit Uncle many times as an adult. She became a mother with three cubs of her own. She would bring the cubs to the cabin and lay to the side and the cubs would romp, run and play with the children and the dogs. The cubs came and went into the house and followed the children every step.

This day the bear brought the cubs to the cabin but did not come out into the open. She kept to the trees and kept the cubs with her. Uncle told the young men the story of the orphaned bear and that she brought the cubs to visit. He made it clear that they were safe as long as they did not try to hold the cubs. He made that statement many times, as the cubs wandered out of the trees to play.

They ran and romped with the children and the dogs for some time, and then their curiosity about these three humans sitting around the fire got the better of them. They wandered about sniffing the air and checking them out. The young men were enthralled with their presence. The cubs wandered closer and mamma bear gave voice signals which the cubs did not listen to. Uncle told the boys to not touch the cubs, just let them be. After a while they would wander off on their own. One of the cubs smelled a piece of food by the leg of one of the boys and he nudged his leg trying to get it. The boy reached to get the morsel to give it to the cub. It scared the cub and he squealed. The mamma came running at full gate across the opening and raised up onto her back legs, when she got to the boy she slapped from right to left. The boy's head went rolling down the hill. The blood was spurting out of the top of his body in long shoots.

His body was just sitting there, and the blood was spurting out. The mamma bear made a great loud roaring and started to run off, with the cubs following her. It all seemed slow motion and nobody moved for a very long time. Uncle finally moved and stood up. He started to chant the native tongue and cried. Aunt sang with him and cried also. The other two boys just sat there in a trance like state and did not move for the longest time. Uncle told them that he had to go get the law and for them to not leave until he came back. There was a long span of time that nothing made sense and there was a lot of times when the air was heavy, and the songs were sad.

Daddy came walking out of the trees and stepped up onto the porch. He was tired from walking and sat down without hugging anyone. Uncle walked up and greeted him. He called to us and asked us to come to him. The girls were told that they were going to live on the farm with their grandpa. Even though they had been happy there before, they did not want to leave this place.

“In the morning, let me know your love for I put trust in you. Make me know the way I should walk to you. To you I lift up my soul.” (Psalm 143: 1-11)

Life on the Farm

Life on the farm with Grandma and Grandpa was animals, working the crops, preparing food for storage and keeping the place tidy, a full time job. Work would start at 4am. Feeding the livestock, milking took up time until breakfast.

Grandma got out of bed every morning and cooked meat, fresh biscuits, eggs, and had it ready when they finished the morning chores. After breakfast the girls would walk to the bus stop to go to school.

School was held in a two room building with all the grades taught there. There were two teachers and learning was happy. The teachers always found some story to tell, that brought smiles and laughter. They make learning a game and life was good. All the children thrived and enjoyed going to school. School for the youngest girl was an enjoyed event. She was quick to grasp the lessons and she excelled right along with the other children. The oldest girl could not get it, she was always struggling and kept getting disappointed. The teachers spent a lot of time with her and some children spent time with her also. She learned but at a very slow pace. At night the youngest girl would help her with her homework and play games with her as the teachers did, she was accepted and grew along with the rest of the children but didn't excel.

After school one day when the girls came home, there was a very tall man dressed all in black sitting on the porch with grandpa. He was a neighbor and a preacher. He wanted the girls to come and go to church with his family.

The girls started walking across the ridge on Sunday mornings and walking to church with the neighbors. As they walked they sang, and the music floated across the hills and was beautiful. It took the girls a while to learn the words, but they joined in and soon were singing along with the others as they walked. The man in black talked and told stories from the Bible. The girls loved it and looked forward to Sundays and going to church. Grandpa and Grandma never went to church. Neither did the woman or daddy. It was never questioned and never talked about around the dinner table. The one thing the girl could never understand about the stories the Preacher told, were how come there is such a loving God, but He won't stop the abuse and the beatings.

"Keep me from the way of error and teach me your law. I bind myself to do your will; Lord do not disappoint me." (Psalm 19 25-32)

The Beatings from Grandma

The beatings from Grandma were not as bad as the ones from the woman and daddy. Grandma was mad all the time and when she hit the girl it was hard blows. She always used a limb from the apple tree nearby. It took a while, but the girl soon recognized that the beatings from grandma would occur after she wet the bed or would laugh too much. For some reason grandma did not like laughter, neither did the woman. The one thing that the girl remembers vividly about living with grandma and grandpa was grandma beating grandpa with a broom handle.

There was a woman that lived over the ridge that kept her cow in grandpas' barn. She would come over the ridge twice a day to milk the cow, Grandpa would always send the girls out on a chore or tell them to go play. The one spot they enjoyed playing make believe was a short way from the barn and along the road that went across the ridge. They had constructed a playhouse there and spent time making believe. This particular day the woman came to milk, left and went back across the ridge. A little while later grandpa drove by in his farm truck. Grandma was not far behind carrying her broom. She looked funny walking real fast up the road and the girls laughed. Grandma told them to shut up. It was not long until they heard yelling and hollering coming from the top of the hill. They took off running and found grandma beating the heck out of grandpa and the woman. The woman was naked and was jumping around screaming and crying. Grandma yelled, “Get home your old fool”. The woman started running away without her clothes and grandpa got in the truck and started away. Grandma walked back to the house and yelling, and hollering was heard echoing across the meadow. The woman had someone come get her cow and she never came back to the farm.

On Sunday afternoons relatives would come visit and grandma would cook a big meal. You could see the cars coming down the dirt road and grandma would always say "go get a big hen and clean it for me" That job was for the youngest girl and she learned really quick how to do it and did it well. She would wander through the chickens and when she spotted the one she wanted, she would throw food and the chickens would start eating like they were starved to death. She would grab the hen and jerk it as her grandma had taught her and break its neck. Then she would cut open its belly and take out all the guts. Then she would dunk it in the kettle of water that was always setting there over a fire in the yard. She would clean the hens feathers away and cut off its feet and take it to grandma to cook. All the many times that she got the hen she only got the backbone to eat.

In their culture the men would eat first, then the women would eat, then the children would eat. By the time the children got to eat there were not very good Pickens left. After everyone finished eating the girls cleaned up and did the dishes. The youngest girl was always clowning around and making jokes to keep the girls laughing and it was not a hard chore. When all the dishes were done they would go out to the rear of the house and lay around under the tree.

The house had a toilet out to the side of the house. There was a saying "we have a nice house with a path" The toilet was a small structure that had a hole dug under it. There was a seat with two holes cut into it that allowed them to sit over it and relieve themselves. It smelled really bad and grandpa had to put lime on it every week because of the smell. The kids would watch the adults walk back and forth to the toilet. They made a game of how long it would take the adult to do their business and go back to the front of the house. One afternoon Grandpa's sister had come with the others She was a schoolteacher and was so prim and proper. She came around the house in a trot going to the toilet. The kids started laughing and teasing. They knew what was about to happen. After few minutes the woman threw open the toilet door and with her panties down around her ankles started hopping around and screaming. "I'm going to die, I've been bit by a snake, Lord God have mercy I'm going to die".

The men came running around the house and caught her and tried to calm her down. She would not stop screaming. Finally, grandma and the other ladies arrived and got her into the house. You see, an old hen had made a nest in the toilet under the seat. When

Aunty sat down the hen jumped up and pecked her genital area. She was sure a snake had gotten her. The kids got yelled at for laughing so much.

Grandpa had a huge bull and he was gentle unless you tapped him on the snout. He would stand out in the pasture, chew his cud and watch over his girls. There was a pretty good size pine tree that stood just inside the pasture from the house. It was deformed and made a perfect place to pretend riding a horse and playing make believe. The girls had walked across the pasture one day looking for berries. Of course, they found none. While walking back the youngest girl stopped to talk to the old bull. He snorted and she snorted back. He pawed the ground and she pawed the ground. She reached out and patted him on the head and he just stood there. She patted him on the nose, and he snorted. She laughed; sister told her not to do that. She reached out and patted him on the nose and this time he bent his head to the ground and started pawing the ground with both feet. She took off running. The bull came right behind her, bellowing and snorting in a lot of anger. She reached the pine tree and climbed up onto it. She was standing there watching the bull come at her in a dead run. She tried to climb higher into the tree but was not fast enough. The bull hit the tree head on and collapsed into a heap on the ground. This was not funny. She had killed grandpa's' bull and she was going to die. Grandma had heard the commotion and was rushing across the yard to get to the girl. She had been knocked out of the tree and across the fence landing hard on her butt in the dirt. The bull just lay there. He looked like he was dead. She wished she was dead. Oh, golly she hurt. She was scared to death. Then the bull grunted. He opened one eye and grunted again. Grandma was pulling at her to get up, to move. She could not. It was like she was frozen. Nothing worked. Here came grandpa. His long legs were moving fast, and he was puffing and saying words that were not nice. The bull grunted again and tried to move. Grandpa arrived, took one look at her and ran to the bull. He rubbed its head,. moved its legs and tried to get it to turn over. The bull grunted and rolled onto its legs. Its eyes were really funny. They just kept moving around in his head. He kept shaking his head and grunting.

After a while grandpa and grandma were able to get the bull onto his feet and he stood. He stood with his head hanging for a while and then he bellowed. It took a while, but he seemed to be ok and wandered off to his girls. After that the bull would stand in the pasture and chew his cud, but if the girl came into the pasture he would paw the ground, snort very loud and start to run towards her. Grandpa said she had ruined his bull. She had to stop going into the pasture.

“The Lord, The Lord a merciful and gracious God, slow to anger and rich in kindness and fidelity, continuing His kindness for a thousand generations, and forgiving wickedness and crime and sin, yet not declaring the guilty guiltless, but punishing children and grandchildren to the third and fourth generation for their father's wickedness". (Exodus 33 - 34)

The girls were taken back to live with daddy and the woman. They did not know it then, but that was to be the last time they got to see the grandparents. They both died in their eighties, but the girls were never able to get back to them.

“Lord God I take refuge in you. From my pursuer save me and rescue me, lest he tear me to pieces like a lion and drag me off with no one to rescue me.” (Psalm 19B)

When the Girls Got Back

When the girls got back to the house where their daddy lived with the woman, things were not good. Daddy would go to work and the work began, the beatings began, and the hunger started. They were used to eating all they wanted, and they had been happy. The woman was not going to have any part of them teasing around and playing.

She soon put an end to it. The youngest girl was fooling around one day and teasing her sister. They were laughing and playing around out in the yard. One of the next door neighbor girls came out of her house and started to talk to the girls. The first time they had ever talked to the neighbors and it was a good feeling. The woman came out of the house and told them to get into the house. When they got there, they were beaten with the broom handle, the youngest girl was drug around the house by the hair to the basement steps. She jerked open the door and shoved the girl down the steps and slammed the door.

* * *

Daddy had dug out a space about 8 x 8 feet under the house. He cut a hole into his bedroom floor and put a vent there. He then cut a hole in the attic wall and put a vent there. He placed a fan in the attic vent to draw the cool air up from the basement through his bedroom and through the house out the attic, to cool the house. - Twanda

* * *

It was dark under the house, but the vent in the floor gave off a wee bit of light. The girl crawled over to the light and sat there. She stretched out her legs in front of her. She began to notice the smells there, and they were not pleasant. She could hear movement but could see nothing. After a while with her sitting there in the dirt, something moved by her. A snake crawled up to her and then proceeded into her pant leg. She had been told about the copperheads and the rattlers that lived in the mountains and she was scared to death. She had heard her mother pray; she had heard her grandmother pray. No one prayed in this house, but she remembered.

She started saying "God don't let it bite me, please God don't let it bite me". Sometime later a very large snake with a white stripe across its neck crawled over to her and up beside her leg. The snake inside her pant leg came out and it crawled over to the side and curled up. The big snake with the mark across its neck crawled a circle around her and then crawled over beside the other snake and curled up beside it. She did not realize it then but something great and wonderful had just happened. From that day forward when she was sitting there in the little beam of light, no snakes came within the circle that the big snake had crawled about her body sitting there. The young girl was pushed down those cellar steps many times and locked down there for hours at a time.

At this point a little bit of history should be given. When Grandpa (daddy's dad) was 14 years old, he was bitten by a rattler just below the right knee. He had been carrying water to the workman and was walking through or close by a briar patch. He thought he had just been scraped by a briar. While he was sitting with the men resting someone noticed that his leg was black. They ripped pants and found the snake bite. They then caught a rabbit and split it open and wrapped it about the snake bite. He was very sick from the bite, but he survived. It is an old Indian legend that if a rattlesnake bites you and you let it live, you and yours will be protected by its spirit for many generations. They did not find or kill the snake that bit grandpa. AND The mother, the grandmother, the grandfather had prayed and prayed for the health and safety of the girls.

The woman would spend a lot of time sitting at the kitchen table looking at a Sears-Roebuck catalog. She would sit there, pick her nose, eat chocolate covered cherries and drink coffee. Little girl stood in front of her one day and asked if they could have a piece of candy. Whop! She slapped her so hard she stumbled backwards. She was told, the candy was hers and that they were not to touch it. "Hell no, you can't have a piece of candy, it is mine, not yours", you half breed, get away from me, why don't you die, get away from me". Another time the woman was sitting at the table, and the little girl was feeling brave. She walked up to her and asked, "can we call you mother"? Whop! that catalog really hurt as it slapped across the child's face. She grabbed the child by the chin, pulled her to her. With her face close she screamed "No, you cannot call me mother, I'm not your mother, you G--dam half breed, get out of here, get out of my sight, I hate you, why don't you die, get away from me". She sounded and looked silly acting like that, and the child laughed. Oh, Oh, should not have done that. Another chore was added. She was drug outside, pushed down onto the ground and told to crawl and pick up everything that was not supposed to be there. Every twig, every leaf, every blade of grass that was out of place. That yard was the cleanest in town.

I Have Thought and Thought

I have thought and thought about it and I believe that that is the first time that I thought about it being better if I were dead. I, at that time, started thinking about dying and how I was going to do it.

When I would spend time In dwelling on death and planning my demise, I came to believe that if I thought it, it would happen. But, in so doing, I learned to accept my own mortality.

If we were always conscious of the people in our lives and those around us being mortal, and most times being here only by a tiny thread, then we might be more kind, The more loving, more understanding and most of all be more thankful for their very presence in our lives.

Love is as a two edged sword. It punctures, it cuts, it burns. Love like a sewing needle mends the holes in our hearts, closes the gaps of heartache and despair.

Love is a necessary thing. We cannot live without it; we cannot entirely live with it. God, our Creator, does not need me, He wants me. He placed me here on this ole globe for a reason. He expects me to make something of the life He has given me.

He expects me to make this ole world, in some way, a better place by my presence here. God expects me to be better than I was when I arrived here.

I feel sometimes that when I come up to the gate through which He will arrive, that I am nowhere near where I am supposed to be. I feel that I have failed in the job that He has given me to do. That gate does not open onto something divine, but onto something that becomes another challenge in the moving toward a Life with God and eternity. I sometimes view those around me and myself floundering about in life. Then I find myself thinking what must God be thinking watching us in our passing through life. - Twanda

----

"All time is eternally present, leading inexorably to an end that we believe results from our actions but over which our control is mere illusion." (T.S. Elliot.)

“Ghosts do not exist. Evil exists all around us. We have a battle all around us continually between good and bad. But if we do not fear it or the ghosts, then they cannot hurt us. They do not exist. Our fears cause the harm to come to us in just thinking about it.” (Dean Koontz)

Daddy's wife had a lot of things hidden about the house, that daddy did not know about. When he went to work, she would take them out and look at them. She would spread them around on the kitchen table and smile and feel them and look at them. One day I came into the house to see if I could get a drink of water and I saw this pretty shiny thing laying on the table and I picked it up and said "wow, this is pretty. Is it yours"? She took the piece from me and slapped me across the face screaming that it was hers and I was not to touch it. IF I touched anything of hers again, she would kill me. I got a cup and turned on the water to get that drink and she grabbed me by the hair and slung me across the kitchen screaming that she did not tell me that I could get a drink, that if I wanted a drink to go get a drink in the creek. Then she started screaming to "get out", get out of my sight", "just go out and die, get out of here".

Sociopaths cannot open their notes, their keepsakes, or their evil grizzly personalities to our viewing. They have to keep them all hidden away, and only to be viewed by themselves to be caressed and enjoyed in the darkness of their souls for their own private enjoyment. They act on it, and it comes into being. - Twanda

----

“Stand by me God do not forsake me. Do not abandon me, my Savior.” (Romans 3:10)

Another Chore Was Added

Another chore was added when a little baby came into the house. The woman would throw the dirty diapers into a metal wash tub. She filled the tub with hot water and filled it full of dirty diapers. She never rinsed out the poop and threw them in with all the rest. The girls had to kneel beside the tub and rub the diapers on the wash board.

The woman would walk behind the girls and slap them across the back of the head as they knelt there rubbing the diapers. Then they refilled the tub and rinsed the diapers. They then hung them on the clothesline out in the yard. Sometimes they hung the diapers on the line in the middle of the night. When they came home from school, they took down the diapers and folded them. If she left a stain or did not get them snow white, then she would have to redo all of them. She would be pulled out of bed and be forced to wash all the diapers over again. Sometimes it took her all night and she would go to school without sleep or anything to eat. The older girl would be pulled out of bed and made to clean the house all hours of the night, while daddy was at work.

She came home from school one day and the tub was filled to the top with diapers. Where did they all come from? She had rubbed them the day before and they were all clean. The woman had put the diapers in the coal pile and rubbed them around, then put them into the tub to be washed. It was impossible to get the coal dust out of the diapers. The girl was beaten with whatever the woman could get a hold of, slapped across the face, cussed and yelled at because she could not get out the coal dust from the diapers. The baby wore grey diapers for a very long time. (Note that bleach had not been introduced at that time)

When the baby was 1 1/2 years old, she had a horrible accident. There was a new item that came from the Sears catalog and was setting on the side of the stove with the electric cord dangling down between the wall and the stove. The baby crawled over to the area, reached up, took hold of the dangling cord and pulled. The hot boiling coffee came down over her back, shoulders, head and legs.

When they pulled the diaper off the infant body the intestines came out with the diaper. The child was in critical condition and with the many prayers for healing recovered after many months and was left with very thick horrible scars on her body.

Eating was something that caused a lot of anger and pain. The girls went about without eating for long periods of time. They were not supposed to eat anything unless the woman gave it to them. The older girl started stealing raw potatoes and hiding them and when they went to bed, they would hide under the blanket and eat the potatoes. One day the woman was standing on the street talking to neighbors and the girls were hungry. The younger one ran into the house grabbed a slice of bread and put some mustard onto it. She ran out the back door stuffing down the bread. She ran smack dab into the woman coming around the house. She took the remaining bread, opened the girl's mouth, ran her finger down her throat and made her vomit. She caught the vomit in her hand, shoved it back into the girl's mouth and held her nose and mouth shut until she swallowed. She screamed, "I did not give it to you, you cannot have it. You are a thief, I will kill you, do you hear me, if I do not give it to you, you cannot eat it. She was screaming that if she saw me eating anything that she did not give to me, that she would shove a snake down my throat and see how much food I could steal then.

* * *

To this day, I go to great lengths to make sure that my mouth is closed when I sleep, because I do not want that snake going down my throat. - Twanda

----

"God is the shield that protects me. …I will thank the Lord for His justice; I will sing to the Lord." (Psalm 19B)

The Girls Were Required to Walk the Mile Home

The girls were required to walk the mile home each day at lunch time. They were given a slice if bologna between two pieces of bread to eat on the way back to school. Some days they did not get anything to eat. One of these days the little girl down the street came running from her house to the street, just as the girls were passing by. She gave the girl a fried egg sandwich with mustard. That was the best food she ever ate. To this day 70 years later, that was the best food she ever ate.

The girls could only sit at the table when daddy was at home. He would get the best looking food. It looked so good. One day he had a piece of meat on his plate that looked, and smelled so good, it made the girl's mouth water. She kept looking at it and daddy noticed. He cut off a piece of the meat and placed it onto her plate. She took it into her mouth and just held it there. It tasted so good. She wallowed it around in her mouth until she looked in the direction of the woman. She looked like she was going to explode. Her eyes bulged out; her face was so red that it looked like she was going to start bleeding any second. The piece of meat disappeared down the girls' throat and landed in her stomach like a rock. Oh, Oh, daddy please don't go to work. He did. The woman slapped her across the face so hard she fell to the floor.

She pulled her up by the hair and started beating her with the stove wood she had in her hand. Some of the places that she got hit with the stove wood began to bleed. She was hurt so bad, was so sick to her stomach, and was so mad at that point that she could not cry. She just stood there and felt the blows as they came. She realized that the woman was screaming, "Cry dam you, cry". She made up her mind right then and there that she would never cry again. The beating finally stopped, and she just walked out of the house and climbed up the hill behind the house. She went a long way and just sat down. How long she sat there she did not know, but it was a long time. That spot became a safe spot for her. She went there many times after that. Things started to change for the girl that day. Nothing made sense. She could not laugh anymore. Nothing was funny. Nothing mattered.

The girls were not permitted to talk to anyone. They could not play with other children. The woman would walk down the alleyway as the girls walked to school. If she saw them talking to anyone, they would get a beating when they got home from school. If she saw them talking to anyone through the hedges, they would get a beating.

The girls were made fun of and bullied. The other kids thought they were weird and were mean to them. The youngest girl having been treated the worst at home had developed a bad attitude. When the other kids would pick on her sister, or laugh at her, she would try to defend her. Of course, she was seen by the woman in the alleyway and would get a beating when she got home. One girl in particular was excessively cruel to the girls and was always walking to and from school behind the girls. She would make bad comments and throw things at them. After the many beatings and cruelty at home the youngest girl turned. She stopped in the middle of the street, waited for the mean girl to catch up to them, and she grabbed her by her long dark hair and ripped off her clothes. She got into her face and told her to shut up, and stop being mean to her sister. She did not hit her. She turned and walked home. She walked into the house just knowing that today she would die. Nope. The woman just stood there looking at her. She said nothing and she went back to her Sears-Roebuck catalog.

“Stand by me God do not forsake me. Do not abandon me, my Savior.” (Romans 3:10)

When the Girls Lived with Daddy and Her

When the girls lived with daddy and her, if they got to go away from home, they had to ride in the back of the truck. They sat on the floor of the truck and looked out the back, as daddy had built a house over the back of the truck. They were riding in the truck one day when they went through a little town a few miles down the road. Daddy stopped at the red light and then there was too loud, real loud bangs. The girls knew what they were immediately as they heard them all the time. They were gun shots. There was a man on the right side of the street that shot the man on the left side of the street. At the same time the man on the left side of the street shot the man on the right side of the street. It was so slow motion. They just stood there, then they started to fall. So slowly they fell and toppled over into the gutter of the street. Daddy looked out his window and said, "I guess they don't have nothing to fight about now". He put the truck into gear and went on down the road.

“God can withhold nothing from faith and prayer. The atmosphere is so heavily charged with resisting forces for limp, lazy prayers to make headway.” (Brother Drake)

She Was Nine Years Old

She was nine years old when one day one of the Jackson boys crawled under the hedges and told her that her grandmother had been in a car wreck. It scared her because they had been in a car wreck and she was the only one that was injured. That was so scary to her and she just knew that grandma was dead or broken up. She ran down the alley across the railroad tracks, the creek and up the main street to grandma's house. The house was full of people and grandma and her husband were sitting at the kitchen table. They had bandages all over them. But they were sitting there eating. With that she knew that they would be alright, but she still needed to hug them and tell them that she loved them. While she was hugging them, daddy walked through the back door. He told her to go get in the truck. She said, "No. I want to stay here with them". He grabbed her by the arm and pulled her out of the house, down the walkway, across the street pushed her into the truck. The woman was sitting there, and she looked back into the back of the truck with the biggest smile on her face. When he got her home, out came the belt and she got a real good beating all the time listening to "I told you to never go around them", I told you to stay away from them". Ha! that did it for her. Something inside her snapped and she got real mad and she remembers thinking, "ok, I can't go see my grandma, I can't talk to anyone, I can't play with anyone, but yes, I can get beat half to death every day" Something snapped and she got so mad. She ran to her spot on the mountain and sat there, laid on the grass watching the clouds and started plotting how she could make up for all the wrong in her life. She talked to God a lot. Grandma always talked to God, and she told me that Mommy would pray for hours. She said that there would be a puddle of water all around her where she would pray so long and so hard. She said that Mommies' hair would be wet, her clothes would be wet with her sweating, weeping and praying. She wanted to be like her and talk to God a long time and sweat like that. At this ripe ole age, she knows that she is alive today because Mommy prayed through,

----

“Out of the depths I cry to you oh Lord. Lord hear my voice! Oh let your ears be attentive to the voice of my pleading." (Psalm 130)

Granny Prayed for Me

Granny prayed for me. With all that has happened over the span of my life, I know without a shadow of a doubt that God has been by my side each and every step of the way. That leads me to think about the car wreck daddy had. He was drunk on Christmas eve. He told us he would get some fireworks for us to shoot off. Then he got drunk. I was the one that mouthed off and reminded him that he did not get the fireworks. He told everyone to get into the car. We did. The woman started yelling and cussing immediately after the last door of the car was shut. She yelled at me. She yelled at daddy. The more she would yell; the faster daddy would drive. He tried to pass a bus on the main road. He ran smack dab into the back of the bus. The next thing I remember is running around trying to find my sister and my daddy. He was sitting on the sidewalk with a policeman standing beside him. My sister was sitting on the grass away from the road. I do not remember seeing the woman.. Someone stopped me, and held onto me, he put his handkerchief over my face and told me to stop, I had been cut on the chin by the ashtray in the back seat of the car. Poetic justice? Yep, I was the one that reminded daddy that he had not gotten the fireworks. The woman reminded me of that daily and nightly for years. - Twanda

* * *

Every time that she would think about Daddy running into the back of that bus, the girl would get hit with whatever she had in her hand at the time. The girl got really good at passing by her and ducking so that when she would swing she would miss her. She was winning that battle.

“How long, OH Lord will you forget me? How long will you hide your face? How long must I bear grief in my soul, this sorrow in my heart day and night? How long must my enemy prevail?” (Psalm 13)

“It is true, He was crucified out of weakness; but He lives in the power of God. We too, are weak in him, but we live with him by God's power in us. I am broken, crushed to the earth, --- speak Lord, your word of life.” (2 Corinthians 13:4)

One Day Her Daddy Was Sitting on His Haunches

One day her daddy was sitting on his haunches on the street with other men. They sat like that many times just talking. The young girl was sitting behind the hedges in the yard stringing clover blooms together making a necklace. A copperhead snake lay close by coiled and ready to strike. One of the men looked through the hedges and saw the snake. He reached through the hedges and grabbed the snake and drug it through the hedges away from the girl. They killed it and came to check out the girl and see if she had been bitten. They could not believe that she was ok.

Sometime later the neighbor across the street was out in his yard. A big rattler with a white stripe across its neck was laying in the sun in front of the girl's house. The man yelled and went for something to kill it. The girl sitting stringing clover blooms saw the snake and yelled for it to leave. She screamed "he is going to kill you, leave, run away". The snake ran back under the house. He was safe. The girl got a beating for chasing away the snake. Needless to say, the jig was up, her sneaking and stringing clover blooms was over.

"God deals with us, simply by just making us wait. He increases our desire, which in turn enlarges the capacity of our soul; making it able to receive what is to be given to us." (St. Augustine 1 John)

Wetting the Bed

Wetting the bed became an everyday occurrence. She tried everything she could think of to not wet the bed. The mattress became soggy and smelled terrible. She still had to crawl onto that mess and sleep. (many years later the girl wondered why the woman did not put a pad on the bed as Auntie had done) A pot was brought into the house for nighttime peeing and pooping. It helped some. At least the bed wetting did not happen every night. Guess who had to empty and clean the pot even though everyone used it. You got it. some nights she would sit on the pot and fall asleep. I guess the thought was that if she sat on the pot, the pee would go into the pot and not on the bed. Hmmmmmm Ok, bad idea. One night she fell asleep sitting on the pot, and it had been used a lot. She fell off the pot, the pot turned over and spilled all over the floor. She woke in a fright. The scream, the slapping, the whipping was nothing to having to clean up the mess spilled on the floor. She never slept on the pot again. She did however tie her foot to the bottom of the bed. The foot turned black, the foot hurt, and she cried. Did not do that again either. Every time that she wet the bed, the woman would beat her, daddy would come home from work, take off his belt and he would beat her. When he was drunk he did not know which end of the belt he held, and the buckle would hurt worse. The belt prong would stick into her and when he pulled it back the blood would spurt out. Those little white scars on her body came from the belt prong. One-day daddy was drunk, and he stated that if she did not stop wetting the bed, maybe she could learn by running to the end of the street without clothes on. Yep, you got it. The very next time that she wet the bed the woman ripped off her clothes when she came home from school and whipped her all the way to the end of the street and back. That good looking boy across the street just stood there with his mouth hanging open. She had grown hair and her boobies were beginning to show. Yep she ran to the end of the street naked. She did not stop wetting the bed.

“Guard me as the apple of your eye, Hide me in the shadow of your wings from the violent attack of the wicked." (Psalm 17)

The Girls Were Not Permitted

The girls were not permitted to see their mother's mother. She lived in the same town and a short distance away. At one of her birthdays, I cannot remember which one, Grandma, Mother's mother baked and brought her a cake. The girl was crawling around on the lawn picking up things that did not belong there. There could not be even a little blade of grass that had turned color allowed to be there. Grandma's husband parked the car on the sidewalk in front of their house. Grandma called to her to come there. She walked up to the car and she was sitting there holding the prettiest thing she had ever seen in her life. It was a very big cake, it was white, with red decorations all over it. Grandma said, "Happy Birthday, Honey." She then held the cake out the window to the girl. She was so happy. She got a birthday cake. It was all hers. It was made just for her. Gosh, that felt good. To her knowledge, that was the only cake that she ever got as a child. She stood there, holding the cake and looking at it. Grandma was talking to her, but she did not know what she was saying. She kept talking and the girl just stood there holding the cake and feeling so good. The woman came to the door and started screaming at Grandma and her husband to get out of there. She cussed, she screamed, and she yelled for the girl to get into the house. She does remember Grandma and her husband telling her that they loved her. Then they drove away. The girl carried her beautiful cake into the house. When she got to the kitchen table, she put her cake on the table and just stood there. The woman came up behind her, grabbed her by the hair and started hitting her with a piece of wood that she had picked up on her way back into the house. She kept screaming things like, "you little whore, you accept gifts from people", I will tell you what you can get from people, I will tell you who you can talk to." She screamed and cussed and kept hitting her across the shoulders and back, then she hit her on the legs. I can see her standing there in the middle of the kitchen looking at her beautiful cake and the woman screaming and hitting her. The woman then picked up the cake and carried it to the back door. She walked out the door, onto the walkway, and then threw the cake as hard as she could out into the yard. She was screaming all the time that she would teach her what she could take from people. She would kill her if she took anything else from anyone. She then walked back into the house and told her to get out of her sight. She screamed, "just die, get away from me." The girl went out to the cake splattered on the ground and started putting her finger into the frosting and licking her finger. She sat there beside her cake and ate the cake until she started throwing up. After that, she climbed the hill and went to her spot on the mountain. She lay there on the grass and watched the clouds float by and she listened to the birds. She listened to the little squirrels scurrying all about. She listened to the train connecting to the coal cars. She listened to the whistle calling the men to come to work and telling the men working that it was time to quit for the day. She listened to people living. She listened to people doing what they had to do to live. She laid there in the grass and became another person that day. To this day, she cannot receive anything from anyone. It makes her angry to have to stand, sit there and have someone, anyone try to give her something

----

"Lord, arise, confront them, strike them down! Let your sword rescue me from the wicked; let your hand O Lord, rescue me from men, from men whose reward is in this present life." (Psalm 17)

One Day a Man Came to the Door

One day a man to the door selling encyclopedias. He and daddy sat on the steps outside the front door talking for a long time. At the end of their talk daddy bought a full set of the books. A glass door cabinet came with them. Sometime later the girls came home from school and there were the books setting there in the living room. Since they could not touch anything in the house unless the woman suggested it, they moved on, changed into their ragged clothing and went to work. Sometime later a teacher in school gave instruction for the class to write a report on topics the teacher gave to each of them. They were instructed to look up the topic in books to glean information to write about. One of the boys in class asked if they could use the encyclopedia to do the report and was told to do so. She said that was an excellent way to get info. The young girl went home, changed her clothing and did her chores. She then went and sat down in the floor and opened the door for the encyclopedias. She found the topic she was given and started to read. The woman had walked up the street to her friend's house and when she came home she saw the girl curled up on the floor reading one of the books. She grabbed the book, yelled, cussed, grabbed the girl by the hair and pulled her to her feet and started slapping her across the face. She used the book and hit the girl everywhere she could with the book. All the time screaming that she was not to touch the books. They were her ooks and the girl could not touch them. She screeched that if she ever touched the books again that she would kill her, her sister, and her daddy. The girl never even looked at the books again. When she went to school she used the encyclopedias there to do her work for school.

"Keep me from the way of error and teach me your law. I bind myself to do your will; Lord do not disappoint me." (Psalm 19 25-32)

Daddy Would Go to Work

Daddy would go to work. He worked the evening shift for many years, then he worked the midnight shift. On the midnight shift, he would leave the house about ten o'clock. She was in bed most of the time, by the time that he left the house. The woman had a sister, that spent a lot of time at their house. When Daddy left for work, they would come into the girl's room and start playing with her. They would touch her, stick their fingers into her and laugh. Laugh, she hated that laugh. She would fight to try to get away from them, but she was a kid and they would hold her down. It hurt really bad when they would stick things up into her. She bled a lot and sometimes, she had to stuff her panties with rags, or tissue to keep the blood off her clothes. She peed when they were playing with she and the woman beat her with a little baton that was laying nearby. She hit her on the shoulders with that baton and the next day, she had the darkest black, purple she ever saw. She told kids at school that she was trying out something for Halloween.

* * *

I was a child; I grew up without the love of a mother or a father. I never got a hug. I never had a playmate. I never had someone to help me with the homework. I remember the first time a boy put his arms around me. I was at school, standing on the playground in front of the front doors to the school. IT was cold and I was there without a coat, and I was freezing. The doors did not open until a certain time either in the am or at noon. We had to stand outside in the elements until that door opened. One of the boys, that I later was to realize was quite a wonderful person, came close and put his jacket around me and wrapped his arms around me. My first instinct was that of joy. It felt so good. Then I heard HER voice. If she saw that I was talking to anyone, let along having someone touch me, I would get a real beating. I shrugged out of the jacket and ran down the steps to get away from him. I remember standing there with goose bumps all over my arms and legs, and my teeth chattering so bad, they made a loud noise. I looked up at him standing there above me and he put his jacket back onto his own body. I wanted to run back to him and ask him to put his arms around me again. But I knew if I did that, I would get a beating when I got home. I remember to this day the joy that I felt when that young man put his arms around me. It is one of those special times in my life, that I hold dear.

Watching children brings about a certain feeling of nostalgia, sentimentality. We seldom see the toughness, the endurance and the strength that children possess. I have read that from birth to the age of 6, children learn all that they need to live their lives. The rest is just filling in the spaces in the grey matter and creating awareness in dealing with day to day ordeals.

In a Dean Koontz book, I read that the past and the present are present in the future, and the future is contained in the past.

I lived in the past. I lived in the then future. I now, looking back can see where the three time periods were the same. You just have to cross the lines drawn in the sands of time, to be able to look back and see how you crossed them. - Twanda

----

"Stand by me God do not forsake me. Do not abandon me, my Savior." (Romans 3:10)

There Was a Dream That She Had for Years

There was a dream that she had for years, over and over. She was in her spot on the mountain, lying in the sun, when this big black bear would come and sit beside her. He would stick his paw into her, and it would feel so good. It would tickle. After many years, she learned that the bear came to visit her in her dreams when the woman and her sister would come and "play" with her. She had not had that dream in years. One thing that she does notice, is that every time she sees a bear, or hear of one, she gets that tickle. On one of those nights that the woman and her sister were with her, they were talking about wanting some "wacky weed". The woman told her sister that she could not take any more money right now, she thought that he was getting suspicious. The sister laughed, clapped her hands, and said "you have friends, use her (pointing to the girl) she can get us all kinds of the weed. Use her". After that many times, a car would show up out front, when Daddy had left for work. The woman would take the girl to the car, the man would hand her some money, and he would take the girl somewhere and touch her. He would put something into her, that hurt really bad, and when he grunted and make weird noises, he would put that thing back into his pants and take her back to where the woman would be waiting.

Sometimes the man would make her put her mouth on that thing and yell at her to suck. He would hold her head and sometimes, she would vomit and sometimes she could not breathe. That would only cause him to stick it into her pee pee hole. She learned that that was really wrong when she met the Priest She did not know that what they were doing to her and with her, was wrong. On one of the days that the woman put her into a car, there were three men. They drove to the top of the mountain and did their thing with her. When they finished, they drove back down the mountain, they stopped in front of the school and opened the door and pushed her out of the car. Of course, she fell and skinned her knees. She did not know what they were going to do then, and she got up and started running. She ran away from the car, and that took her up the hill towards the churches. She ran until she could not get her breath and just fell against the stone of the building of the church. She slid down the side and put her head onto her knees. She was so out of breath, she was gasping. She started to cry. Someone sat down beside her and put their arm about her shoulders. They pulled her towards them saying, "awwwwww missy".

* * *

That is all, just those two words. She does not know how long she sat there, but I do know that was the first time that she discovered that there was someone that would not hurt her. -Twanda

* * *

The man in the black dress was the Priest of the Catholic Church at that time. She had always been told that the Catholics were bad people and that she was to stay away from them. When she stopped her snotting and snorting, she looked up into the eyes of someone that knew that she needed help. That help came to her in many sessions before school and after school teaching her about our Almighty God. He introduced her to a Nun who taught her that she was loved, and she taught her that she was an unruly and needy person. She taught her that she could be loved. that she was loved.

After she left her daddy's house, she went to the Catholic Church and discovered that Jesus loved her. The Priest never said or did anything out of the way towards her. The Priest and the Nun hugged her and made her feel special. Those were the only hugs the girl got until she ran away from daddy's house. To this day she remembers that she could trust them in anything. He smelled of wine and he smelled of smoke, but he walked with God.

* * *

Oh yes, I am sure that he had his faults, we all do, but there was something about this man that took her under his wing and taught her about God. -Twanda

* * *

He taught her that the things that were happening to her were wrong.

* * *

The priest became a part of the lives of a lot of the kids in the camp. The boys would dam up the creek and we would all enjoy it. On a hot day the priest walked up to the pool of water took off his shoes and swung out over the water and make a big cannon ball. From that time, we went roller skating, sledding, and ball games all the while learning about the stories in the bible. The priest was one of us, he taught us a lot. He taught me that God loved me and that God had created me special as He did all of us.

I chuckle when I remember his 25th Jubilee. The Bishop was processing into the church and we were in the choir balcony. We made a game out of making little balls out of tissue and dropping them down to see if we could hit the heads of the choir boys processing into the church. This day I had a handful of little balls and just as the Bishop passed underneath us, I dropped. The ball of paper landed on the Bishops head. Sister Angela used the long limber rod that she kept close by and whacked us all across the shoulders. When Bishop removed his hat the little ball of paper rolled down his body and onto the floor. He just looked up to us and just a hint of a smile crossed his lips.

Later that day, when he confirmed me to become a Catholic, he mentioned being bombarded by the paper wads and tapped me on the cheek with his hand and told me "yep, you are going to make a good catholic

The only real peace that I have, Dear Lord, is in You. Through all life's frustrations, pain, and heartaches, I keep running to you.

- Twanda

The Beatings Became Worse

The beatings became worse, the yelling, screaming and violence were just about all the time. The girls came home from school one day, walking into the house to see the woman fly across the room and bounce off the wall. She and daddy physically fought a lot. Furniture was broken, black and blue showed up on both.

At one time the skin coloring in the residence were shades from black to a beautiful yellow. The woman had placed a small bed on the front porch, and that is where the girls were to sleep. Oh yes, she left open the door sometimes in the winter but not always. There was no heat out there. That is where the woman told them to go once she got up off the floor. Her nose was bleeding, and she had pooped on herself. She looked disgusting. Daddy was laying on the couch, and he just turned over and went back to sleep.

Nothing else happened that night, but the next day when the girls got home from school, daddy had gone to work. When the girls saw his truck missing from the driveway, the girls started crying. They knew what was in store for them. Instead of going to the house they crawled through the hedges and sat against the wall where she could not see them unless she walked around the house. It was not very long until she came looking for them. She had a broom in her hand, and she started swinging when she got within range of them. The older girl got hit on the head and she went down. She was out cold. The younger girl saw her sister go down and was not moving. She stopped running and turned on the woman as she closed in on her. She grabbed the broom and twisted it out of her hands and started hitting the woman just as she had hit them over the years. She hit the broom on the ground and broke it. The woman was rolling around on the ground and begging for the girl to stop. The girl stuck the broken broom handle under the woman's chin and told her, "if you lay another hand on either one of us, I will ram this stick up into your brain", and then I will stick it up your ass, just like you did to me". the woman's eyes were red, wide and really not focusing. The girl screamed "do you hear me. do you understand"? She shook her head "yes" and started to get up off the ground. The girl pushed her back down and stuck the stick under her chin again and informed her that she was not just kidding around this time. She meant ever word she was saying." With that the girl shoved the stick into the ground beside the woman's ear and screamed "do you understand me"?

Well that was that. let the battles begin. At that moment there was a loud sound of applause and cheering. The neighbors had witnessed everything that had happened and apparently they enjoyed the show.

Things were very quiet and peaceful that night. The next day when the girls came home from school, daddy's truck was in the drive. Yippppeeee they thought. When they went into the house he took off his belt and proceeded to beat them in turn. The youngest girl looked over to the woman and she had that smile on her face. The girl had stopped crying a long time ago when the beatings occurred. She asked the woman "you like what you see, what you cause"? "You did not believe me did you"? At that point the girl grabbed the belt that had just landed a blow across the back of her sister, jerked it and it became hers. Daddy was not too steady on his feet when he was drunk. She threw the belt to the side and informed them that that was the last beating they would get. Daddy jerked her, shook her, and proceeded to hit her in the mouth. She went out instantly and landed with a thud onto the floor. When she woke, she was laying on the kitchen floor in a pool of gelled blood. Her eyes were so swollen she could barely see. She could not breathe through her nose; her maxillary front teeth were embedded in the roof of her mouth. She just lay there. The woman and daddy were sitting at the table She could not hear what was being said. Everything was muffled. After a while she got up off the floor and went to the toilet, then she went to find her sister. Sister was laying across the bed just staring into space. There were no tears.

“Lord do not let my lying foes rejoice over me. Do not let those who hate me unjustly wink eyes at each other.” (Psalm 35:27-28)

The Next Day

The next day daddy had to take the woman to the "store". Grocery. It was 5 miles away in the next town. They pulled out of the driveway. The youngest girl age 15, told her sister that she loved her and always would, she started walking. She walked about 6 miles going in the other direction from where the woman and daddy had gone. Her first cousin pulled beside her as she walked on the side of the road. When she turned to look to see who was talking to her, he went ballistic. He demanded to know who had done that to her. She had to write it as she could not talk very well. He took her to her grandmother's house. It had been a very long time since she had been there. When they saw her, they started weeping and wailing. Someone yelled, "call the sheriff". Someone cussed and grabbed his gun. Someone screamed "get her to a doctor". About that time the cousin asked someone coming into the house "do you know who did this to her, did you do it or did that witch of a woman you married do this to her"?

Daddy jerked off his belt and was stepping towards the girl, and instantly three men stepped between them. He was told that he would not live very long if he hit her again. Daddy told the girl to get into the truck, she was going home. She shook her head grunting. Cousin picked up a coke bottle and stated that daddy needed some come uppance. The other two men escorted daddy to his truck and followed him back to his house. It is interesting that the older sister never got another beating She did however move in with a family down the road a piece, not long after that.

* * *

Here I want to state for the record, that daddy had been drug out of the house a short time after that and when they brought him back, he was a bloody mess. Another time everyone was awakened in the middle of the night by a huge cross planted on daddy's front yard was burning brightly. The other interesting thing that happened is that somehow a wild cat got into daddy's house and the woman was badly injured when she tried to remove the cat. -Twanda

* * *

The younger girl lived with her grandmother and cousin for two years. She went to another town to help care for a newborn and help out. After the newborn was older and the mom could handle things, the girl got a job in a restaurant. Not much pay but she was paying her way.

"When it is time for me to punish, I will punish them says the Lord." (Exodus 32:34)

There Are Voids

There are voids many voids in her life. The doctors say it is called depression, with traumatic amnesia. There were not many doctors. When she got sick she was told "you will either get well or you will die". There were many times that she thought that she would die. Later in life she decided that the reason they were not allowed to see doctor, was because of all the bruises and sores. She sits and wonders if she will ever remember the lost years, if she will survive the memory. She has been told that if she is hypnotized, and gets memory replaced, she may not handle the events very well.

* * *

So, in that light, we shall continue on with what is remembered. Not in any sense of chronological order. - Twanda

----

“Guard me as the apple of your eye, hide me in the shadow of your wings from the violent attack of the wicked.” (Psalm 17)

Remember the Boy

Remember the boy that took off his jacket and wrapped it around her shoulders. He wrote her a letter when she was living with her grandmother. He had joined the Navy and was stationed on a ship. They wrote back and forth and when he had leave from his duties he came home. The two were joined at the hip. Then he had to go back to his duties. He sent her a ring and asked her to marry him. She was told no, "you are too young, and you do not know what life is really all about". The boy sent her a ticket and she went to California on a Greyhound bus. She had 33.00 dollars in her pocket and absolutely no fear. She rode that bus for three nights and three days. He met her at the station and took her to a friend's house. She was to help out with the three kids in exchange for a place to live. The two foolish kids went to Tijuana Mexico, signed some papers and were told they were married. The girl had been to one wedding where they stood before a preacher and exchanged words while they were married. That is what she wanted and was told, "we are married and that is that". He shipped out to sea for 6 months and the girl was left to baby sit. Life was good. She had her own bed to sleep in, she had an indoor toilet, with a bathtub. There was all the food that she wanted and spending time with the children was wonderful. She ate a pizza. Yum. She went to the beach and had the time of her life. The older child taught her how to ride a board and in turn ride the waves into shore

She learned how to drive by driving Her "husband's car" up and down the street where she lived. When she felt that she could drive with her eyes closed she put on a sundress and went to get a license to drive. She had never heard about parallel parking, so she failed the test. Parallel parking became the activity of the day. Every free minute was spent parallel parking. She went back to take the test again and this time she only had to parallel park and she was on her way home in half an hour with a driving license in her pocket.

The boy came home from his tour of duty and they immediately started driving to visit with their families back east. It took them four days to make the drive. and she slept almost the entire way. When they arrived at his aunt's house (she ran a boarding house and was the only one with a room for them to sleep) he slept, and she helped cook and clean. After a week they were on their way to his next post.

They settled in a small garage type house with apartments upstairs and down. They were given the downstairs one. The girl that lived in the upstairs unit was a wonderful cook. She made an apple pie and asked the girl to come eat a piece. The girl had never heard of an apple pie and did not know what it was. It was the best thing she had ever put into her mouth. She set about making an apple pie. HAHA not going to happen. What a mess. The boy took one look and laughed. Not gonna do that again.

She had a lot of time on her hands and took walks and went fishing in the small lake out back of the house. She had a string and used a stick pin, which she had bent as gear. She caught fish and sharing her catch with the kid's upstairs was a real joy for her. One day while she was lying in the grass watching the clouds roll by. She started to think about the many times that she lay in the grass on the mountain watching the clouds. The sounds were the same, the sights were the same, but life was so much better. One warm sunny day she lay on the grass and went off to sleep. She awoke to a noise close by. That was something she had never heard before. When she got the courage to open her eyes, there was a creature staring down at her. What the hell is that? She was so scared she could not move and asked God to help her. The thing moved his head and blinked its eyes. She blinked her eyes. What was this thing? It moved in slow motion and it was not long before she realized that she could move fast enough to be well away from it before it could do anything about it. When she had scooted a distance, she looked upon her first big turtle. He was so big that a small child could sit upon his back. When the boy returned home that evening she took his hand and practically drug him to see the turtle. It was not there, and he laughed. They got to see many large turtles after that.

The girl talked to the girl upstairs, asking her about her wedding. When she listened, the girl realized that she was not married. She asked the boy if they could get married in the church.

His response was that they were married and to shut up about it. She had learned from the priest at home that having sex without marriage was a sin. After practically begging to have a formal wedding and the exchanging of vows, she decided that she did not want to live like that. She got on a Greyhound bus and moved on.

"I can do all things through him who strengthens me." (Philippians 4:13)

The Girl Joined the Navy

The girl joined the Navy. She had to take two courses to meet the graduating (from high school) credits she needed. When the courses were complete she was sworn in as a member of the United States Navy. She went to Bainbridge Maryland for training. That was fun. She marched, went to class and ate. There was food everywhere. She gained 18 pounds in three weeks. She was called into the office and had her eating habits curbed. After all they had issued uniforms and she was soon to grow out of them.

She went to another base for further training. She learned how to care for the sick. She learned that the abuse she had suffered as a child was wrong. She spent many days and sleepless nights wondering why no one stepped up to help her and her sister. Where was her sister, was she still alive? She went to another base and worked in the hospital there. The Vietnam War was in full swing and she decided that she wanted to go there. Nope. Women could not go into combat. Women could not be married. Women could not be pregnant. She went to another place to work.

At the new base there was an amusement park a short distance away. There was a large hill, green grass that looked and felt like a carpet. On the 4th of July that year, she took a blanket and settled on the grass to watch. Just as the fireworks were about to begin, a sailor squatted down beside her and asked if he could join her. She told him "no". He persisted and put something to her throat. She told him to go away and to leave her alone. He still persisted and told her to get up and come with him. She said, "God please help me". Two times she heard "Fall back". Two times she did not listen. He was persistent. The little voice said, "Fall back". That time she listened and fell back onto the ground. The knife caught her on the jawbone and cut a 4-inch gash. A sailor sitting next to her jumped to his feet and pushed the man to the ground. He sat on him and slugged him a couple of times asking for others to help him and get someone to help the girl. Someone grabbed. her and drug her off to the side. They put something to her jaw and held tight. The fireworks were so beautiful, and the bangs and booms were deafening. The MPs came and cuffed the sailor and took him off. The Medics came and took the girl to be stitched up.

The Navy did not like the messed up mouth of the girl and ordered her to the dentist. That led her to a surgeon who spent 4 1/5 hours picking out the pieces of splintered bone and teeth from her pallet. A bone graft was placed in the area and she was sent off to heal. After healing they made her false teeth and all she could do was sit with a mirror and admire her new face. Such vanity. The bone graft did not take, and another surgery was performed to remove the decaying bone. She had a new opening of her mouth, but it was not pretty. Oh well. We should not be vane.

There is a memory of the girl standing in an office. There is a Priest seated behind the desk. She has told him that she wants to get out of the Navy and get married. He is angry and very unhappy. He is telling her that she cannot do that. If she does that she cannot enjoy the sacraments. He stands, swipes everything on the top of his desk in one fell swoop onto the floor. She stands and moves toward the door. He continues to yell, cuss, and tell her that she is throwing her life away, that he is not Catholic, and she cannot marry him. He slams his fist into the wall and leaves a dent. She is waiting for the blows to come her way. They don't. He yells for her to get out of his site and that if she marries this man and still goes to communion that she will die.

"Put no trust in princes, immortal men in who there is no help. Take their breath, they turn to clay and their plans that day become nothing." (Psalm 146)

She Marries the Man

She marries the man because he treats her like a queen. She did not know about love; she had never experienced that emotion. He spends money on her and dotes on her, causing her to feel things she has never felt in her life. She feels an emotion that is foreign to her. They are married by a Methodist Preacher in his office. She moves in with the man, who has moved to Connecticut for a new and higher paying job. Two weeks' after getting there he comes in drunk and accusing her of things she knows nothing about. He calls her a liar, throws her onto the floor. He straddles her body, holding her down. He slaps her, he slugs her with his fist and continues yelling and cussing at her. He starts yelling for her to fight, when she does he rapes her. When he is finished he rolls over onto the floor and says, "Damn that was good".

When he went to work the next day, she went to the doctor. She had a fractured jaw and they wired her jaws together. She knew that she could not stay in the hospital, so she went home and went to bed. She had dinner on the table when he came home. His words to her were "behave yourself and keep your mouth shut and that won't happen again".

She had an ectopic pregnancy, which ruptured, requiring surgery and 3 units of blood.

His job took him away from home 3 to 4 weeks a month. When he was away, she worked at a job, worked around the house. She was always alone except while she was at work.

She had another pregnancy which resulted in a still birth. She named him Stephen and buried him.

She was pregnant again and this time it was a miscarriage.

He came home from one of his trips and drank until he was very drunk. He threw her onto the floor and proceeded to beat her and rape her again.

He is away when she delivered this child, who is also stillborn. When he is called to be informed about the event he is drunk and laughs it off stating that it is her bad stock that these children are choosing to die rather than to live and be with her. She put a little pink bow in the baby's hair and named her Suzette Michelle and buried her.

The man's job took him all over the states. He was always going abroad to Japan, Spain, and Europe as well as others, wherever the job took him. Just about every two years there was a new address for them to live. A number of the places they lived are totally wiped out or memory. Her life consisted of beatings, ridicule and dying babies. She had a big change in her life when the man kidnapped his son from another marriage and brought him to live with them. The boy was young and just about as scared as the woman was. He talked little and ate a lot. The man gave her 60.00 a week to feed them. She got no other money than that. She wore clothing that she made herself, while the son wore the best there was to buy. She would find fabric on sale and make it into something to wear. The woman had to pay the utilities from her check.

When they lived in Connecticut the fabric cost 25 cents a yard in the outlet stores. Their home was custom Homemade curtains, cushions, bedspreads, pillows. even sheets to match were clearly displayed and used. As long as she kept her brain busy, all the rest did not matter.

He came home from a trip the second time they lived in Connecticut. She received the beating and rape and life went on. She already knew that everything that happened, was her fault. He yelled and told her that she was nothing, she was from eastern Kentucky and she was nothing. She had heard it enough and learned to keep quiet and not to rock the boat. She enrolled the son in sports to get his horizons opened and to help him find a way to feel good about himself.

Another pregnancy. No joy there. She did not get excited about it. She did however ask God to help this child live so that she could have someone to love her.

The girl child was born and went directly into the Nicu. She fought and fought and with the help of almighty God she got to live and be held by her mother. Her name was disputed and argued about for days. The woman wanted Elizabeth to be a name for her. That would make five Elizabeth's in succession on her side of the family.

After days of the father making a total fool of himself the name was recorded. His mother's name, Name from the bible (he had to have it that way), Elizabeth and that was that.

“The Lord said: "Fear not…I am with you" (Acts 18:9-10)

The Child Grew

The child grew and became for the most part a very healthy baby until the age of 10 months. They traveled to his parents' house for the holidays. No one had said anything about them having Hong Kong flu. When they were there two days the baby got sick, she had a fever and started grand mal seizures. She was rushed to the nearest hospital. There they did not know immediately what her problem was and admitted the child for further tests. She was placed in isolation and the only way the mother could see her was to stand in the hallway and peek through a slat in the blinds, of the window to the room. The mother would not leave the site, she stood there the rest of the night and up into the next day. She was silent most of the time. She was so tired and so sore from standing there she began to weep. All the hurt, all the pain, all the humiliation of her life spilled out onto the floor there in the hospital peeking into the room where her only interest lay, hooked up to wires and hoses.

The hospital was operated by a group of nuns of the Catholic faith. One of those nuns walked down the hallway as the woman stood there sobbing her heart out. The nun put her arms around the woman and attempted to lead her to a seat. No, that was not going to happen, the woman was staying there and watch her only child. The woman got back some composure and told the nun about her daughter being there all alone. The nun started to pray, and the woman joined her in familiar prayers. When all was quiet again the nun excused herself and walked away. After a while the nun returned and with her in tow was a nurse with a gown, a mask and a smile. The woman was draped masked and led into the room of her daughter. When the child saw her mother, she stood up on the bed and reached for her mother. She spends a few more days in hospital, but mom was right there with her.

About three months after they returned home to Connecticut, the child woke them screaming. She was having another grand mal seizure. She was rushed to hospital and after an hour or so, the doctor told the mother "you might want to hold her, she may not make it until morning". Mom sat there and told God that she could not live without the child. The next morning the child was chipper and playing.

Four times afterwards the child was laid in her mother's arms and was told that she might not make it until morning. When they lived in Dallas the doctor told them that he did not understand how the child was still alive after another grand mal seizure. He advised them to take the child to Yale New Haven Children's where they were doing research in infantile seizures.

They went back to Connecticut and this time he rented a house on an island just off the coast. It was beautiful living there. She could fish every day but with the child every day was just not possible. They took the child to Yale New Haven Children's and the child was turned inside out. The people there were going to find out what was causing all the seizures. In the end, after a week of tests and questions the verdict was in. The man had a defective gene that caused the seizures. It was genetic. It was something that happens when family marries family. The man was certainly not the woman's family. She wanted to beat him as he had been beating her, it was about this time that the woman reached the point that somehow she did not hear of nor see any other woman getting treated as she was being treated. She started questioning that. The child was put on three medications to stall seizures. All three had bad things to watch for.

"Lord I take refuge in you, from my pursuer save me and rescue me, lest he tear me to pieces like a lion, and drag me off with no one to rescue me." (Psalm 7)

Since They Lived Along the Shore

Since they lived along the shore the man had to have a boat. His friends all had boats and he bought one. He told the woman that she could not go anywhere on the boat without him, and that she had to take a course in how to maneuver a boat. She signed up and proceeded to attend class. One evening when she was about 3/4s through the course she looked out the window and saw her husband standing there looking into the window. After a few minutes he turned, walked to the car, where the child was waiting and drove away. When class was over he was there to give her a ride home. He started asking her about her boyfriend. He wanted to know how long the affair had been going on. When she tried to defend herself saying that there was no boyfriend, he backhanded her with his closed fist. It knocked her out and she fell against the window and .... nothing. When she woke from the hit she was lying in a heap in the floorboard of the car. The car was in the driveway where they lived. When she was able to do so, she opened the door of the car and slowly maneuvered her way into the house. The child was in her playpen; he was watching a football game on TV. She checked the child and went into the bathroom to wash off the blood. She could not open her mouth. She could not focus. He came into the bathroom and grabbed her by the chin, he was in her face and was telling her that he would not stand for her to cheat on him. He was spitting in her face as he talked. She could not talk with his holding her jaw so tight. He drags her into the bedroom and slapped her, yelled at her, and raped her again. This time, once again she heard him say "dam that was good".

“God is the shield that protects me. Psalm19B. I will thank the Lord for His justice; I will sing to the Lord Highest Praise.” (Psalm 19B)

The Men Were Going Fishing

The men were going fishing. The woman loved to fish and asked if she could go along. The other man said that was a wonderful idea, that they would not drink so much if she came along. She was permitted to go along with them. She had never been on a boat before at least not to go out into the bay. The world looked different out there. It was beautiful. They showed her how to rig the pole and how to put on bait. The bait was a 6-inch fish. What kind of fish could she catch with that? She did as she was instructed and before they could get a line in the water she hooked a big fish. She got it into the boat and baited her line, dropped it to the bottom as she had been told. A few minutes later she hooked another big fish. This was fun. This made her happy. After bringing in three big blue fish she was told that was the limit, she could catch no more. As they fished she sat and watched the birds, the clouds and noticed that the water was getting rough. The boat would slide down a swell and the water would be 20 feet high above the boat, the boat would ride high on a wave and the water was 20 feet below the boat. She was having the time of her life and was laughing and bouncing around like a rubber ball. The men decided that with the water getting so rough they would go into shore. It was an interesting ride as she had never been out on the water when it was rough. That night she cleaned the fish as she was the only one that caught any. The man came into the kitchen and wanted to know how long she had been sleeping with his buddy. She laughed. He slapped and yelled, he drags her into the bedroom and slapped, yelled and raped. The next day he put padlocks on the outside of the doors. He told her that she could not go anywhere unless she went with him. He took the phone when he left.

Sometime during this period of time, he went away on a four-day fishing trip. The child went into grand mal seizures. The woman opened the windows and screamed to the neighbors to help her. The EMTs arrived and took the child to the hospital. The doctors brought the child to the mother and suggested that she hold her. As she sat there that night, she sang, she hummed, and she prayed. She remembered that the Blessed Mother could help her, and she asked her for her help. She talked to Jesus, she talked to God. That night she got some backbone avowed to Jesus, Mary and God that she would do whatever it took if they could spare her child. About 5am the child opened her eyes and smiled. Since the child had vomited on her, and bled from biting her tongue, the woman had to get a shower and bathe the child. A policeman drove her home and suggested that she call the Coastguard and tell them that the man was needed at home. It was the pleasure of her life to make that call. About 9 hours later a car drove into the yard and two men in uniform half drug the man into the house and dropped him onto the bed. They made a report of the padlocks on the doors and left. The man woke but there was no fuss. He did not yell, he did not slap, nothing, He just turned over and went back to sleep.

"Oh search me, God, and know my heart. Test me and know my thoughts. See that I follow not the wrong path and lead me in the path of life eternal." (Psalm 139: 23-24)

At a Time When the Temps Were Warm

At a time when the temps were warm and the sun was shining, the woman filled a child's pool with warm water for the children to play. There were children at the adjoining properties that would come and play with the little girl. The woman had cut off the end of the hose as the children would sling the hose around and when it hit them it would hurt. That day the children had been playing for a good while and the man came around the side of the house. He had a drink in his hand and told the children it was time for them to go home. When they left he told the child to go into the house and put on some clothes. The woman started to pick up the toys and empty the pool. The man threw her down onto the ground face first and proceeded to sit on her. She was struggling to get up and he kept hitting her in the back of the head, telling her that she had to pay for cheating on him. He pulled off her clothes and stuck the hose up her rectum. He laughed as he slapped her across the back of the head. and when the water and feces started coming out her mouth and nose, he got up off her. He yelled ": holy shit" ran to the car and left. The neighbor saw what had happened and helped the woman into the house. She wanted to call the police, but the woman knew that would do no good, so she begged the neighbor not to. The neighbor stayed with the woman for a while and played with the child while the mother showered and put on clean clothing. The woman vomited many times during this process, and she was so weak she could hardly stand. After a while she stopped vomiting and stopped going to the bathroom, and the neighbor made them some tea and after the woman was calm she went home.

"Praise be God, the Father of our Lord Jesus Christ, the Father of mercies and the God of all consolation! He comforts in all our afflictions and thus enables us to comfort those who are in trouble, with the same consolation we have received from Him." (2 Corinthians 1:3)

There Is No Memory of the Man Returning

There is no memory of the man returning home after this incident. They did move to New York after this event. The man put a deposit on a house that was under construction. They lived in a motel waiting for the house to be ready to move in. The day he was to go close on the house, he changed his mind and bought a mobile home. It was parked beside a golf course, so that he could play whenever he wanted. Things were good for quite a while. The children were doing great in school. There was no yelling, no slapping and no disruptions at all. Then one cold day in January the man came in from being gone for two days. He did not say a word, he took her by the back of the neck and pushed her into the bedroom. There he threw her onto the bed and straddled her. He slapped, He punched he yelled. This time she fought back. she bit him. she raised her knees and shoved him off her. He came back with a vengeance, he pinned her into the bed and raped her. His words that day were "dam woman you are learning really good". "That is the way it will be from now on". She cleaned herself up, made dinner, bathed the child, went into the bathroom and swallowed 200 Atropine tablets. There is no memory for five days. The woman woke to a Bare room with a mattress on the floor, and nothing else. The nurse came in seeing that she was awake and told her she was lucky to be alive. Shit!!!! She was dammed.

Her heart had stopped, and she was zapped to keep her heart beating. There is a memory of beauty, very white light and people moving around. She saw her grandmother, but she was pushing her away. Grandmother told her to go back, she could not come to be there now. There were the sounds of birds singing, beautiful music and little babies smiling at her. Everyone in the light were happy and she wanted to stay with them but could not.

She was kept in the hospital for 14 days under the vision of a lot of people, there was a Head Doctor, a Priest, and wonderful nurses. The woman learned through listening and watching that the way her life had been lived was not the way it should be, she learned that she had value and that NO ONE had the right to lay a hand on her. Through the Priest she learned that God really did love her and wanted her to be a happy person.

"God has given us the wisdom to understand the mystery, the plan he was pleased to decree in Christ." (Ephesians 1:3-10)

One Afternoon

One afternoon the woman was sitting in the reading room and a woman came to visit her. She said the Priest had asked her to come. They talked and the visitor made a statement that the woman did not understand. She asked the visitor to repeat what she had said. She said, "life is wonderful if the man and the woman are in sync. If they are then sex can be 100%. The women can be happy, and the man most certainly can be happy". OK what does your happy mean? The visitor went on to state that if the man was gentle and caring enough the woman could climax and enjoy the sex also". NO ONE had ever talked to her about sex before, Sex to her was something the man did, and she had to pay for allowing him to do it. This caused a whole other way to think. When she went home, the man sold the mobile home and bought a house. It had a pool, a large family room and three bedrooms. Nice, but too late. There was nothing to hold the woman any longer. She was growing stronger every day. The more she listened in therapy the stronger she became,

One evening the woman and child were in the den before a beautiful, warming fire reading. When the child was younger the woman never got to read to the child. To be honest she did not really know that she was supposed to read to her. No one had ever read to her. She did not have contact with anyone to learn what she should do and shouldn't. It came bedtime and the woman was carrying the child, both of them laughing, and as she approached the top the man was sitting on the steps. The woman said, "excuse us" and looked up. "She was looking into the barrel of a 38 snub nose pistol. He told her to just say one word, that is all it took. She said "go ahead, shoot, but... you better be sure I am dead.

The child started to cry and the woman told him "go ahead you bastard shoot".

"What, are you a coward now" He pushed her aside and left the house. The next day he came home sober, with a bouquet of flowers. The woman took the flowers and threw them into the garbage. He started to talk, made himself a drink and leaned on the counter. She was preparing a turkey for the oven as the next day was

Thanksgiving. He stated very clearly "You are beautiful, and I love you, but I want a divorce". She stood there for a couple of minutes, put her hand on the iron skillet on the stove and began to laugh. He just stood there. Then he asked, "What the hell is the matter with you, did you hear what I said".

Her response was "Yes, I heard you", as she gripped the handle of the skillet and swung with all her might. It hit him on the side of his skull, and he collapsed in a heap on the floor. The children came running and asking what was wrong with daddy. The woman poured a cup of coffee and patiently waited for him to either wake up or die. He woke and started crying. She laughed. He literally crawled, falling a lot, to the bedroom and crawled up onto the bed and collapsed again. She did not look in on him again but went about her business. For three days he slept went to the toilet, got a drink and slept some more. When he was able he took a shower and sat down at the kitchen table. He was informed that he could have his divorce. He got expensive lawyers and got a divorce. He was only to pay $50.00 a week support. The son was to go with the daddy. (The boy then moved in with his girlfriend in Connecticut) The woman, for the first time in her life felt a sense of freedom. She worked 3 jobs for six years to keep a roof over their heads. Oh No, ... the child was very well taken care of. The man doted on her and she got everything she wanted or needed.

* * *

I think sometimes that everything that has happened to me in the course of this life has been my fault. I caused it to happen, I was there at the wrong time, the wrong place. How can one rationalize a bad thing that happens to them as being all their fault? While I was married to R.E., everything that happened was my fault. If the sun came up, it came up the wrong way. If it rained, it rained too hard, too long, not enough. If he had to work overtime, it was my fault. As it was all my fault, he had no problem with finding an opportunity to punish me. - Twanda

* * *

The EX got his divorce on a Wednesday and he married his new gal on Friday. He did not know that in the state of New York, you could not marry for 6 months after a divorce.

Of course, she did not tell him that. It was her little secret. The new wife had a house and a Cadillac which he drove all the time when he was in town.

He would show up everywhere the woman was and want to talk. She avoided him in every way she could, but sometimes he was just a leach and she could not get by him. She was having lunch with a friend one day and he walked into the restaurant and just sat down with them. After a while the friend left stating that her food was not sitting well with her. HA! After she left he reached over to take her hand in his, and stated that he wanted her and the child to move to Houston and he would buy a condo for them to live in. He said that she would not have to work and that she could have free travel to anywhere she wanted to go. The woman began laughing and could not stop. She laughed until tears ran down her face. He could not see the humor. He was serious. She stood up when she had gotten her composure and gave him the ticket for lunch. She walked out the door, up the street and went back to work. He continued to show up and it was such a nuisance she just picked up, packed up and moved to Miami.

"A pure heart create for me O God, put a steadfast spirit within me. Do not cast me away from your presence, do not deprive me of your Holy Spirit." (Psalm 51)

She Did Not Like Miami

She did not like Miami, did not like it one bit. She had lived there before and did not like it. Why in the world did she go there again? Oh yes, she took the child to all the attractions, enjoyed the beach, and kept busy. She just did not like the heat, the sand, and as far as she was concerned there was no true North, no true South and where the hell was East and West? Every time she started some place she had to stop and ask directions. She had lived all over the states and here in this dreadful place she could not acclimate. The EX was showing up in Miami just like he did in New York. When he was not on a job abroad, or tied to a project in the states, he would appear. She likened his appearances as to the little mole sticking his head up here and there. She wished it were so and that she had a very large mallet. She packed up one day and started back north. She made the trip enjoyable for the child in that they stopped often and enjoyed the sights along the way. She had friends in Harpers Ferry West Virginia, and they stopped to visit.

After being there for two weeks she decided to just get a job and stay for a while. She rented a cottage on the banks of the Shenandoah River and went to work in the local Hospital. The child settled in well and the woman kept her active in church, school and friends. There were friends from school, and church that just about lived at the cottage. There was swimming, bon fires, trips to D.C. hikes, wiener roasts and sleep overs that seemed to be the way of life. The children were happy, they could be trusted, and they were growing and having fun. On one weekend all the children, who were from 11 years to 19 years were spending the weekend with the pastor of the church. They had some type of project and they all decided they would help. That particular weekend a young man that worked at the hospital asked the woman to join him in exploring the festival in the area. That was interesting, and they walked along the Eyrie Canal for six hours and talked and talked. After six months the man convinced her that the child needed stability and that he could give her that. They married. The child who was 11 years old hated the idea and became a snot.

The woman was sitting on the porch reading and the phone rang When she answered the voice was familiar. It was her sister. It had been twenty-three years since she had heard that voice. She was stunned into silence. She could not form her words. Only guttural sounds came out. Her sister was living in Baltimore with a couple and the friend had looked up the woman and called her. They spent a lot of time together and gradually became comfortable. Sister had had a hard life and had failed pregnancies just like the woman. Sister had two bad marriages, which ended in divorce. Sister had two children, one died when she was 3 months of age, the other lived, and was 20 years of age. Their lives were almost parallel to one another. There were a lot of occurrences' in their lives that were almost picture. They spent hours just talking.

"Gird the loins of your understanding; live soberly set all your hopes on the gift to be conferred on you when Jesus Christ appears." (1 Peter 1:13)

The Man Wanted To Go Back To School

The man wanted to go back to school and get his masters. After checking around, they decided that he could go to University of Kentucky and they could be close to family and friends. They could also be within driving distance of his family in another state. Life was good. The child settled into school and joined the school band. She loved it. The man worked and went to school. The woman worked and kept up the house and everything else making it possible for the man to go to school.

The man suffered from PTSD from being a medic in Viet Nam. He had nightmares, and you could not touch him if he was reading or asleep. You would get slugged. He was kind, but he never got excited about anything. He never laughed. He worked, went to class, sat in his chair, read, watched TV and slept. They rarely saw one another. He never talked to her about anything. Once she booked a trip across country via Amtrak. For ten days they were enclosed in a cubicle, on the dining car, or sleeping in bunks. Maybe he said ten words, the entire trip.

"The gift from God. No eye has seen it, it has no color. No ear has heard it, it has no sound. It has not entered man's heart; man's heart must enter into it." (Augustine)

The Child Grew and Became a Beautiful Woman

The child grew and became a beautiful young woman. When she was 20 she came down with idiopathic thrombocytopenia. Yep, don't know what causes it, don't know where it came from. The doctors treated it by taking out her spleen. For twelve days the woman sat at her bedside and prayed and promised God that she would be His slave if he would just let her live. She recovered and came home. The girl became infatuated with a young man and wanted to marry. The couple were engaged, broke up, engaged and broke up a few times. The woman sat on the stairs with the girl for two hours pointing out the warning signs and thought she had talked the girl out of marrying the young man. NOPE. In her opinion the two were just too young to get married. The next morning, they went before a judge and married. The wedding dress had been paid for, taken back, paid for and taken back four times. Deposits had been made; flowers had been paid for. They married; the woman cried.

A child was born to the young'uns and the woman watched the child from the time of birth until the age of 8 years. She watched the second grandchild for 5 years from birth. She loved the children and doted on them. She spent a lot of time just being with them.

"Keep my eye from what is false: by your word, give me life. Keep the promise you have made to the servant who fears you." (Psalm 119:33-40)

The Silence Became Worse

The silence became worse. The man started meeting with friends and drinking. He would have spent days, evenings with friends "just talking". He could not talk to her, but he could talk for hours with his friends. The woman would take the children to the man's place of work and have lunch about once a week. One day, the children were especially happy to be going to have lunch with "Bopp". They cleared security and walked to the dining room. There were a lot of people there and it took a minute to locate "Bopp". Over in the back corner, against the wall, he sat holding hands with a nurse that worked there. A number of diners saw the expression on the woman's face as she turned, with the children and walked out.

There is a long span of time here that is not remembered. The next memory is of the woman coming home from a ceramics class to the sound of muffled sounds coming from her bedroom. The man and the nurse were in her bed, in her bedroom, in her house, naked. No memory.

The woman went through the motions. She had to have done so, as things got done. There was just no memory of having done anything.

"Keep me from the way of error and teach me your law. I bind myself to do your will; Lord do not disappoint me." (Psalm 19 25-32)

The Woman Had Gotten Into Genealogy

The woman had gotten into genealogy and started spending a lot of time trying to find kin. She had grown up without even knowing who her relatives were. When she located someone, it was such a feeling of belonging, or being a part of something. She went to reunions and Melungeon Meetings and met hundreds of people that she was related to. She belonged, she related. She was happy. She went to visit people just to look upon them because they were her relatives. This is the first time that she came into contact with the green eyed monster called "Jealousy." The women started making comments, laughing at her and just being mean with their words. Since the woman had grown up without learning any social graces she was a sitting duck. She felt hurt and just did not know how to deal with strange people being mean to her. She became deeper engulfed in depression. She became even more isolated. She became angry. The nurse that had been found in her bed started showing up at different times, different places and that made for angrier feelings. It was as though the nurse was a ghost and she would just show up in the living room, in the back yard, in the front, just anywhere you looked. She would just be there and then she would walk away. When the woman tried to tell about what was happening, they would not believe her. After all, she was depressed. She had PTSD; she was mental.

“May you attain full knowledge of God's will through perfect wisdom and spiritual insight. Then you will lead a life worthy of the Lord and pleasing to Him in every way. You will multiply good works of every sort and grow in the knowledge of God. By the might of His glory you will be endowed with the strength to stand fast, even to endure joyfully whatever may come' giving thanks to the Father for having made you worthy to share the lot of the saints in light. He rescued us from the power of darkness and brought us into the kingdom of His Beloved Son.” (Colossians 1:9b-13)

Halloween October L998

Halloween October 1998,. She was chatting with her kin, and the Melungeons on the internet. The man was laying on his bed reading. She had been sipping scotch and enjoying the exchanges. She felt funny, she made a comment to her cousin in Baltimore that something was wrong. The cousin told her to go wake her man and have him get up with her. She went to his bed and woke him asking if he would get up and be with her. He turned over, patted her on the leg, saying, "You will be alright".

She went back to the computer and told the cousin what had happened. The next thing she remembers is the nurse standing in the doorway of the room smiling at her. THAT is all she remembers until two days later she wakes up in the hospital with tubes, lines coming in and out of her body. She is told that she had shot herself. She goes back to sleep. She wakes again and is told the same thing. This time she sees her friend walking into the room pushing an IV stand hooked up to him, caring a basket of flowers. He walks over to the back side of the bed, sits down and says, "well they didn't kill you."

She is transferred to another hospital because she is a suicide risk. HA! If she was going to shoot herself, she would put the barrel of the 357 under her chin and pull the trigger. A belly wound is too long suffering before you die. She is not an idiot. She develops an embolism in her lung.

She requests to meet with the attending surgeon that pulled out the damages from the initial wound. He tells her that he had to get tough with her to make her live. She had died and he would not let that happen. He said that she kept saying "just let me go" "please just let me go". He said that at one point he had to mark the time, but still fought her in bringing her back to life. He and the other surgeon stated that "there is no way in hell, that you could have pulled that trigger". The bullet went into her body just above the pelvic bone and travelled in an upward motion through her body and lodged in the damaged muscle in her back. The surgeon had to cut out the bullet, as it was held very tightly by the damaged muscle. He also stated that that was a good thing, if the bullet had exited her body, she would have died and stayed dead. OK, the husband has convinced the police that she pulled the trigger. They believed him. It is written SIGW on the paperwork. HISTORY. But she knows.!

Ok long story shortened and lost somewhere in the grey matter enclosed within her skull, are days, months, of just doing what needs to be done. She asks husband what happened that night, he just looks at her. He will not talk to her. She gets disability because she is "crazy". "She shot herself". Ha! She goes downtown buys the divorce forms, fills them out, pays for them to be filed, and goes home. She is granted a divorce without the man even coming to appear. He has moved in with the nurse.

“You must know your body is a temple of the Holy Spirit, who is within the spirit you have received from God. You are not your own. You have been purchased at a price. So glorify God in your body. (Corinthians 6:19-20)

The Woman Has Now Been Ostracized

The woman has now been ostracized by her daughter for 16 years, she says she needs to be put into an institution and on medication. She had threatened her with jail if she comes into contact with her grandchildren. Yes, the woman has tried to see the children but to no avail. The woman has missed out on all the growing up events of the grandchildren, she has missed it all.

* * *

This is as accurate as I can make it without giving names and wasting a lot of time making statements that has no business being made. I end it here, but it is not over. It will never be over as long as she breathes and walks these hills. - Twanda

* * *

“What we await are new heavens and a new earth where, according to his promise, the justice of God will reside. So, beloved, while waiting for this, make every effort to be found without stain and defilement, and at peace in his sight. Consider that our Lord's patience is directed toward salvation.” (2 Peter 3:13-15)

In Order For Us To Feel a Sense Of Belonging

In order for us to feel a sense of belonging, we must be able to accept ourselves. We must acknowledge our being and how we got to the place where we now dwell. To recognize all the hurts, all the heartaches, all the pain and starvation that we have had to endure during the course of our lives makes us who we are today.

Some of us have had it terribly bad, some of us have had it wonderfully good, and some of us have had it mediocre. Through each experience that we have had to endure, we have grown. We have accomplished the completion of trials and graduated to a higher plane of being. We all must complete something in our lives. We must endure and complete tasks in order to gain the place that we are destined to be. When we do that, then we can claim the pathway to God. Living our lives, enduring life makes us ready to grow to God and what He has planned for us.

Jesus is nailed to the tree. He is hanging there with his shoulders out of socket. In order to take a breath, he has to use his feet and legs to push up so his diaphragm can expand to drag in air to his lungs. His feet are nailed to the tree with one on top of the other. His head droops forward as he has no strength left to hold it erect. The wounds on his body are seeping and pouring out blood, serum, mucus an life causing fluids. The blood has clotted and is drying in the heat of the day. His open gashed wounds are void in most places of wet blood and they appear as ashen spots all over his body. His kidneys give up and the urine runs down his legs onto the dusty floor. His bowels give way and you can smell the waste as it slowly makes its way to the ground. You can hear no talking, birds singing, or men boasting. It is silent and Jesus, my God, my Savior states "it is finished". A guard stabs a blade into the chest of Jesus. Water that has collected in the cavity of the chest of Jesus spurts forth, with a bloody tinge and falls to the ground. The human body of Jesus, the Christ is dead.

I am not worthy of this sacrifice. I am not worthy of one drop of blood that has fallen from his body. He did this for me. He received over a thousand blows to his body, and he hung there on that tree and he died, left His human body and died for me.

I thank you, Jesus, but that is not nearly enough from me. Even the very best that I can do to live a good life, talk good, show kindness, sharing of what I have, helping all I can is not enough. Therefore, I must try each day to be the best that I can be. I must in every way, all that I do show to the world that I want to please God and show it in such a way that every time someone looks at me, they can see Jesus in me.

When I was a child and sitting on the porch of Uncle Jeb and listening to his words, listening to the words of Grandpa on the farm, I was growing. I did not realize that at the time. I realize it now. Once I was told to "shut up and listen". I learned to listen. I learned to hear what I was supposed to hear. Now when I listen, I hear with such a sense of understanding that to tell about it, would surely cause the listener to question me. Others that I come into contact with have never learned how to listen.

Therefore, I am the strange one. So, I keep it to myself. I talk to God about it. I listen and one day I will be able to discern the message that is being meant just for me. - Twanda

----

"May all the peoples of the earth know THE LORD IS GOD and there is no other." (1 Kings 8:60)

* * *

God created we humans all special. It does not matter where someone lives, how they live, how they CHOOSE to dress, what restaurants they CHOOSE to dine in, or what church where they CHOOSE to worship OUR GOD. We are all GOD's children and HE loves us unconditionally.

They mocked, tattled, judged, and shunned, Jesus. He has borne it all. There is nothing a Human can do that has not already been done to Jesus. The thing that really bothers me is how can we be so cruel to one another.

When I got cancer and had surgery and chemo, I did it alone. I survived it with the presence and help of Jesus by my side. - Twanda

----

"Our help is in the name of the Lord, who made heaven and earth." (Psalm 124)

* * *

I have had 24 surgeries. I, at one point, could not lift my head from the pillow, after having four surgeries in one year.

The Bible talks from cover to cover about how the tongue is a two edged sword, how it is a poison and can kill.

I talk to God about it all. I am putting together this book of my life and how so very mean God's creations can be, praying that there is just one person that can benefit from it. If there is just one person, that is not shunned, gossiped about, or turned away, then I did something. If there is just one tear that does not fall, then I did something. IF there is just one child, teen, senior citizen, daddy, mother that has a good exchange from it, then every slap, every beating, every rape, every gossip, every hungry moment, will have been worth it all.

Put your whole trust in God, talk to Him as you will your spouse or best friend. If you give God your happiness, your disappointments, your trials, or when Life just kicks you in the bum you will gain, receive more and more strengths to deal with it all. God is there to help you. Just lift it up and give it all to God. He loves you and wants you to be happy and stronger with-in yourself.

I am praying for you, I am lifting YOU up to God and asking Him to cuddle you in His loving arms, and keep you safe, healthy and happy.

Holy Father bless this brother and or sister, cause them to gain a closer walk with You. Help them to reach out to you and come to know and understand that they are special and that You want them to know all the joy, the peace, the love that only comes from You.

"May you attain full knowledge of God's will through perfect wisdom and spiritual insight. May you walk worthily of God and please him in all things, bearing fruit in every good work and growing in the knowledge of God. May you be completely strengthened through his glorious power unto perfect patience and long suffering; joyfully rendering thanks to the Father who has made us worthy to share the lot of the saints in light. He has rescued us from the power of darkness and transferred us into the kingdom of his beloved Son, in whom we have our redemption, the remission of our sins." (Colossians 1:9b-14)

* * *

Jesus paid it all. Jesus wept, he bled, his body purged on the cross in front of the whole world to see. HE paid it all. Can't we just try; can't we just make the effort to do it Jesus' way?

GOD bless you and please seek for and come to know the PEACE OF CHRIST. - Twanda

----

"Every time we turn our heads the other way when we see the law flouted, when we tolerate what we know to be wrong, when we close our eyes and ears to the corrupt because we are too busy or too frightened, when we fail to speak up and speak out, we strike a blow against freedom, decency and justice." (Robert Kennedy)

About the Author

Twanda Smith was born in Lynch, Kentucky. Lynch at one time was the most productive, populated mining community in the world. People came from all over the world to work there.

She grew up, all up and down the Blue Ridge Mountains, living with family and friends. Having lost her mother to death at the age of three, and her father, not being strong in the parenting aspects, she grew up an orphan alongside her older sister. She developed a strong faith in God at an early age. She clung to and grew strong in the ability to survive, with the presence of God, in situations unbearable to the common populace. Twanda's education has been classroom, and life experience. She attended school while she worked to support herself. Her School of Hard Knocks has provided her with many trophies and medals. Having lived in every section of the States, she settled in Danville, Kentucky in her senior years and enjoys the peace and quiet of the small town atmosphere. In younger years, she kept busy working with Hospice, Red Cross, Local Health Department - Emergency Responders, Pioneer Playhouse, Civitan Clubs of America, and Volunteers in Missions, having traveled with 9 mission trips. She presently works with the Volunteers of the local hospital.

www.ingramcontent.com/pod-product-compliance
Ingram Content Group UK Ltd.
Pitfield, Milton Keynes, MK11 3LW, UK
UKHW041936190726
13854UKWH00004B/1614

9 781716 124464